THE
SUPER DUPER TRIVIA BOOK

Volume 1

APPLESAUCE · PRESS

KENNEBUNKPORT, MAINE

CONTENTS

CHAPTER 1

Sports & Other Games

BASEBALL

1. Five men have hit 60 or more homers in a season: Babe Ruth, Roger Maris, Mark McGwire, Sammy Sosa, and Barry Bonds. Place them in order of how many career homers they hit.

2. In 2010, what Phillies ace became the second pitcher to throw a postseason no-hitter?
   a. Joe Blanton
   b. Roy Halladay
   c. Cole Hamels
   d. Cliff Lee

3. What team was once known as the Colt .45s?
a. Arizona Diamondbacks
b. Houston Astros
c. Kansas City Royals
d. Texas Rangers

4. Effa Manley is the only woman in the Hall of Fame. What role did she play in the game?
a. owner
b. umpire
c. inventor of the box score and several statistics, including RBI
d. composer of "Take Me Out to the Ball Game"

5. What three brothers played the outfield together for two innings in 1962?

a. Felipe, Matty, and Jesus Alou
b. Ken, Clete, and Cloyd Boyer
c. Joe, Dom, and Vince DiMaggio
d. Ed, Jim, and Tom Delahanty

6. True or false? Connie Mack managed the Athletics for 50 years.

7. What happens if a runner is hit by a batted ball?
a. the runner is allowed to advance a base
b. the batter is called out
c. the runner is called out
d. do-over

TOUGH TRIVIA CHALLENGE

8. Who hit the "Shot Heard Round the World" to win the pennant for the New York Giants in 1951?

9. IN 2004, WHAT TEAM BECAME THE ONLY TEAM TO LOSE THE FIRST THREE GAMES OF A POSTSEASON SERIES AND COME BACK TO WIN?
A. BOSTON RED SOX
B. CHICAGO CUBS
C. NEW YORK METS
D. NEW YORK YANKEES

10. In 2004, what team became the only team to win the first three games of a postseason series and lose the next four games?

a. Boston Red Sox
b. Chicago Cubs
c. New York Mets
d. New York Yankees

Did these Hall of Famers ever win a World Series (yes or no)?

11. Vladimir Guerrero
12. Chipper Jones
13. Jim Thome
14. Ivan Rodriguez
15. Ken Griffey Jr.
16. Pedro Martinez
17. Randy Johnson
18. Frank Thomas
19. Barry Larkin
20. Jim Rice
21. Tony Gwynn
22. Cal Ripken Jr.
23. Kirby Puckett
24. Reggie Jackson
25. Carl Yastrzemski
26. Don Drysdale
27. Hank Aaron
28. Ernie Banks
29. Whitey Ford
30. Sandy Koufax
31. Ted Williams
32. Joe DiMaggio

33. What Hall of Famer was nicknamed "The Splendid Splinter"?

a. Joe DiMaggio

b. Sandy Koufax

c. Mickey Mantle

d. Ted Williams

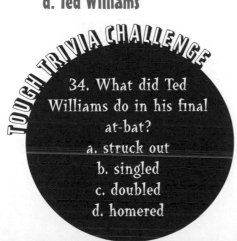

TOUGH TRIVIA CHALLENGE

34. What did Ted Williams do in his final at-bat?
a. struck out
b. singled
c. doubled
d. homered

35. BEFORE BECOMING PRESIDENT. GEORGE W. BUSH OWNED WHICH MLB FRANCHISE?

A. ARIZONA DIAMONDBACKS

B. WASHINGTON NATIONALS

C. HOUSTON ASTROS

D. TEXAS RANGERS

MATCH THE MEMBER OF THE BASEBALL HALL OF FAME TO THEIR NICKNAME.

36. Mordecai Brown
37. Steve Carlton
38. Ty Cobb
39. Andre Dawson
40. Joe DiMaggio
41. Carlton Fisk
42. Whitey Ford
43. Lou Gehrig
44. Rich Gossage
45. Ken Griffey Jr.
46. James Hunter
47. Reggie Jackson
48. Randy Johnson
49. Walter Johnson
50. Larry Jones Jr.
51. Willie Mays
52. Stan Musial
53. Tim Raines
54. Phil Rizzuto
55. Babe Ruth
56. Ozzie Smith
57. Frank Thomas

a. The Iron Horse
b. Lefty
c. Mr. October
d. The Wizard
e. The Big Unit
f. The Big Train
g. Three-Finger
h. The Chairman of the Board
i. The Man
j. The Sultan of Swat
k. The Georgia Peach
l. Catfish
m. The Kid
n. Pudge
o. Rock
p. The Hawk
q. Chipper
r. The Big Hurt
s. The Yankee Clipper
t. The Say Hey Kid
u. The Scooter
v. Goose

58. What pitcher won 31 games in 1968, the most in the last 87 years, but only 41 more in the rest of his career?

    a. Denny McLain
    b. Doc Ellis
    c. Don Drysdale
    d. Bob Gibson

59. Donora, Pennsylvania, with a population of less than 5,000, is nonetheless the hometown of Ken Griffey Jr. and what other Hall of Famer?

    a. Harry Heilmann

    b. Stan Musial

    c. Al Simmons

    d. Willie Stargell

60. Since 1928, the record for striking out the most times in a career has been held in succession by four Hall of Fame outfielders. Can you name all four?

61. THE LEFT–FIELD WALL IN WHAT BALLPARK IS KNOWN AS "THE GREEN MONSTER"?

    A. COORS FIELD

    B. DODGER STADIUM

    C. FENWAY PARK

    D. YANKEE STADIUM

Match the team to its former stadium.

62. Briggs Stadium	a. Detroit Tigers
63. Candlestick Park	b. Minnesota Twins
64. Hubert H. Humphrey Metrodome	c. New York Mets
65. Shea Stadium	d. San Francisco Giants

TOUGH TRIVIA CHALLENGE

66. What disability did outfielder Pete Gray and pitcher Jim Abbott overcome en route to the major leagues?

67. Which of these Hall of Famers is the only player to win batting titles in three different decades?

     a. George Brett
     b. Ty Cobb
     c. Ted Williams
     d. Tony Gwynn

DID THESE HALL OF FAMERS EVER WIN A BATTING TITLE (YES OR NO)?

68. REGGIE JACKSON

69. ROD CAREW

70. ROBERTO CLEMENTE

71. ERNIE BANKS

72. EDDIE MURRAY

73. JOE DIMAGGIO

74. HANK AARON

75. MEL OTT

76. JOE MORGAN

77. MICKEY MANTLE

78. RICKEY HENDERSON

79. DUKE SNIDER

80. HARMON KILLEBREW

81. RYNE SANDBERG

82. BARRY LARKIN

83. LOU GEHRIG

84. JIM RICE

85. HANK GREENBERG

86. ROBIN YOUNT

87. RALPH KINER

88. KEN GRIFFEY JR.

89. BABE RUTH

90. JIMMIE FOXX

91. MIKE SCHMIDT

92. LOU BROCK

93. YOGI BERRA

94. DAVE WINFIELD

95. JACKIE ROBINSON

96. What Hall of Famer won a batting title in 1968 with a .301 average, the lowest average ever to win the crown?

a. Reggie Jackson
b. Brooks Robinson
c. Frank Robinson
d. Carl Yastrzemski

97. True or false? In 1920, Babe Ruth's 54 homers were more than any other American League team other than his own.

98. True or false? As a pitcher, Babe Ruth once led the AL in ERA.

99. True or false? As a 38-year-old, Babe Ruth pitched a complete game for the Yankees.

Match the player to his best-known uniform number.

100. Hank Aaron	a. 7
101. Ted Williams	b. 45
102. Mickey Mantle	c. 24
103. Lou Gehrig	d. 14
104. Willie Mays	e. 3
105. Pedro Martinez	f. 42
106. Roger Clemens	g. 4
107. Pete Rose	h. 2
108. Babe Ruth	i. 9
109. Ichiro Suzuki	j. 44
110. Ozzie Smith	k. 1
111. Derek Jeter	l. 21
112. Jackie Robinson	m. 51

113. Which of these cities has never been home to an MLB team?

a. Altoona, Pa.
b. Norfolk, Va.
c. Providence, R.I.
d. Toledo, Ohio

114. THE NEW YORK YANKEES HAVE WON MORE WORLD CHAMPIONSHIPS THAN ANY OTHER TEAM. WHAT TEAM RANKS SECOND?

A. CARDINALS
B. DODGERS
C. GIANTS
D. RED SOX

MOVIN' ON

Match the franchise with the city it once belonged to.

115. Arizona Cardinals
116. Atlanta Braves
117. Baltimore Ravens
118. Colorado Avalanche
119. Indianapolis Colts
120. Los Angeles Clippers
121. Los Angeles Dodgers
122. Memphis Grizzlies
123. Oakland Athletics
124. Oklahoma City Thunder
125. Tennessee Titans
126. Texas Rangers
127. Utah Jazz
128. Washington Nationals

a. Baltimore
b. Brooklyn
c. Buffalo
d. Cleveland
e. Houston
f. Milwaukee
g. Montreal
h. New Orleans
i. Philadelphia
j. Quebec City
k. Seattle
l. St. Louis
m. Vancouver
n. Washington, DC

FOOTBALL

129. What team won the first two Super Bowls?

    a. Chicago Bears

    b. Dallas Cowboys

    c. Green Bay Packers

    d. Pittsburgh Steelers

TOUGH TRIVIA CHALLENGE

130. What was Brett Favre's first NFL team?

a. Atlanta Falcons
b. Green Bay Packers
c. Minnesota Vikings
d. New York Giants

Match the legendary coach with the team he enjoyed the most success with.

131. Bill Belichick	a. Chicago Bears
132. Paul Brown	b. Cleveland Browns
133. Bill Cowher	c. Dallas Cowboys
134. Tony Dungy	d. Green Bay Packers
135. Joe Gibbs	e. Indianapolis Colts
136. George Halas	f. Miami Dolphins
137. Tom Landry	g. New England Patriots
138. Vince Lombardi	h. New York Giants
139. John Madden	i. Oakland Raiders
140. Bill Parcells	j. Pittsburgh Steelers
141. Don Shula	k. Washington Redskins

142. In Canadian football, a team can score one point by kicking the ball untouched into the other team's end zone. What is this play called?

    a. Blanc
    b. Bleu
    c. Rouge
    d. Verde

143. Who are the only brothers to both be drafted with the #1 pick in the NFL?

144. WHAT QUARTERBACK "GUARANTEED" A SUPER BOWL VICTORY FOR THE UNDERDOG NEW YORK JETS, AND THEN DELIVERED?

TOUGH TRIVIA CHALLENGE

145. Hall of Fame wide receiver Art Monk is a second cousin of what jazz legend?

Were these Hall of Famers first-round picks in the NFL Draft (yes or no)?

146. Troy Aikman
147. Curtis Martin
148. Fred Biletnikoff
149. Terry Bradshaw
150. Tim Brown
151. Harry Carson
152. Cris Carter
153. Terrell Davis
154. Eric Dickerson
155. Marshall Faulk
156. Brett Favre
157. Charles Haley
158. Marvin Harrison

159. Jim Kelly
160. Steve Largent
161. Ray Lewis
162. Joe Montana
163. Terrell Owens
164. Walter Payton
165. John Randle
166. Jackie Slater
167. Roger Staubach
168. Lawrence Taylor
169. Thurman Thomas
170. Kurt Warner

171. True or false? **There are no undrafted players in the Pro Football Hall of Fame.**

172. Before becoming president of the United States, Ronald Reagan played what Notre Dame football legend in a movie?

a. Grover Cleveland Alexander   **c. Paul Hornung**

b. George Gipp   **d. Knute Rockne**

173. Who led the NFL in rushing yards every year but one from 1957 to 1965?

In the Pro Football Hall of Fame as of 2019 (yes or no)?

174. WR Torry Holt
175. LB Pat Swilling
176. TE Ben Coates
177. Coach Tom Landry
178. QB Joe Namath
179. RB Gale Sayers
180. CB Aeneas Williams
181. OL Steve Hutchinson
182. Coach Bill Cowher
183. RB Edgerrin James
184. WR Kevin Metcalf
185. WR Calvin Johnson
186. RB Earl Campbell
187. RB Fred Taylor
188. QB Donovan McNabb
189. OL Orlando Pace
190. WR Bob Hayes

191. WR Randy Moss
192. OL John Hannah
193. LB Karl Mecklenburg
194. WR Michael Irvin
195. RB Tiki Barber
196. DL Kris Jenkins
197. LB Zach Thomas
198. RB Jerome Bettis
199. DL Richard Dent
200. RB LaDainian Tomlinson
201. TE Mike Ditka
202. RB Roger Craig
203. RB Priest Holmes
204. CB Ty Law
205. RB Ottis Anderson
206. WR Chad Johnson
207. CB Darrell Green

Answers: 142. c; 143. Peyton (1998) and Eli Manning (2004) Their father Archie was the No. 2 pick in 1971.; 144. Joe Namath; 145. Thelonious Monk 146. yes; 147. no; 148. no; 149. yes; 150. yes; 151. no; 152. no; 153. no; 154. yes; 155. yes; 156. no; 157. no; 158. yes; 159. yes; 160. no; 161. yes; 162. no; 163. no; 164. yes; 165. no; 166. no; 167. no; 168. yes; 169. no; 170. no; 171. false; 172. b; 173. Jim Brown; 174. no; 175. no; 176. no; 177. yes; 178. yes; 179. yes; 180. yes; 181. no; 182. no; 183. no; 184. no; 185. no; 186. yes; 187. no; 188. no; 189. yes; 190. yes; 191. yes; 192. yes; 193. no; 194. yes; 195. no; 196. no; 197. no; 198. yes; 199. yes; 200. yes; 201. yes; 202. no; 203. no; 204. no; 205. no; 206. no; 207. yes

208. Which of these Hall of Fame quarterbacks never won a Super Bowl?

  a. John Elway
  b. Steve Young
  c. Dan Marino
  d. Brett Favre

210. Which franchise has the most Super Bowl appearances?

  a. Dallas Cowboys
  b. Denver Broncos
  c. Green Bay Packers
  d. New England Patriots

TOUGH TRIVIA CHALLENGE

209. What team reached four straight Super Bowls and lost them all?

211. As of 2019, what two franchises have won the most Super Bowls?

212. As of 2019, which two franchises have lost five Super Bowls?

213. WHAT FUTURE U.S. PRESIDENT ONCE FILED, AND LOST, AN ANTITRUST LAWSUIT AGAINST THE NFL?

● ● ● ● ● ● ● ● ● ● ● ● ● ●

MATCH THE FRANCHISE WITH ITS ALL-TIME BEST RUNNING BACK.

214. BUFFALO BILLS	A. ADRIAN PETERSON
215. CHICAGO BEARS	B. LESEAN MCCOY
216. CLEVELAND BROWNS	C. JIM BROWN
217. DALLAS COWBOYS	D. TIKI BARBER
218. DENVER BRONCOS	E. EMMITT SMITH
219. DETROIT LIONS	F. WALTER PAYTON
220. GREEN BAY PACKERS	G. BARRY SANDERS
221. INDIANAPOLIS COLTS	H. CURTIS MARTIN
222. KANSAS CITY CHIEFS	I. TERRELL DAVIS
223. MINNESOTA VIKINGS	J. O.J. SIMPSON
224. NEW ORLEANS SAINTS	K. FRANCO HARRIS
225. NEW YORK GIANTS	L. EDGERRIN JAMES
226. NEW YORK JETS	M. JIM TAYLOR
227. OAKLAND RAIDERS	N. DEUCE MCALLISTER
228. PHILADELPHIA EAGLES	O. PRIEST HOLMES
229. PITTSBURGH STEELERS	P. MARCUS ALLEN

Answers: 208. c; 209. the Buffalo Bills; 210. d, with 11; 211. the Patriots and Steelers, with 6; 212. the Patriots and Broncos; 213. Donald Trump; 214. j; 215. f; 216. c; 217. e; 218. i; 219. g; 220. m; 221. l; 222. o; 223. a; 224. n; 225. d; 226. h; 227. p; 228. b; 229. k.

Sports & Other Games • **17**

230. True or false? Hall of Fame cornerback Deion Sanders once played in an MLB postseason game and an NFL game in one weekend.

232. What Hall of Fame wide receiver also won an Olympic gold medal in the 100-meter dash at the 1964 Olympics?
a. Lance Alworth
b. Cliff Branch
c. Bob Hayes
d. Paul Warfield

231. What former Raiders running back and Kansas City Royals outfielder is the only individual to be an All-Star in two different professional sports?

233. Before being selected with the No. 1 pick in the 1983 NFL Draft, John Elway spent one year in the minor leagues playing for which MLB franchise?

MATCH THE PLAYER WITH HIS NICKNAME.

234. Jerome Bettis	a. The Snake
235. Joe Greene	b. Night Train
236. George Halas	c. Captain America
237. John Hannah	d. Too Tall
238. Bob Hayes	e. Mean
239. Elroy Hirsch	f. The Bus
240. Paul Hornung	g. Mercury
241. Ed Jones	h. Joe Cool
242. Dick Lane	i. The Golden Boy
243. Bob Lily	j. Sweetness
244. Joe Montana	k. The Refrigerator
245. Eugene Morris	l. The Big Tuna
246. Joe Namath	m. Hog
247. Bill Parcells	n. Broadway
248. Walter Payton	o. The Minister of Defense
249. William Perry	p. Mr. Cowboy
250. Deion Sanders	q. Bullet
251. Ken Stabler	r. Crazy Legs
252. Roger Staubach	s. Papa Bear
253. Reggie White	t. Prime Time

254. WHAT TWO COLLEGES HAVE PRODUCED THE MOST HEISMAN TROPHY WINNERS?

255. True or false? No college player has ever won back-to-back Heisman Trophies.

TOUGH TRIVIA CHALLENGE

256. Florida State quarterback Charlie Ward ran away with the 1993 Heisman Trophy. But instead of playing in the NFL, he enjoyed an 11-year career in what professional league?

a. MLB **c. NHL**
b. NBA **d. MLS**

257. As of 2019, who has won more games as the head coach at Alabama, Nick Saban or Bear Bryant?

258. TRUE OR FALSE? AS OF 2019, BEAR BRYANT HAS WON MORE NCAA *TITLES* THAN NICK SABAN.

259. True or false? Nick Saban once served as a defensive coordinator under Bill Belichick in the NFL.

MATCH THE STAR QUARTERBACK WITH THEIR COLLEGE ALMA MATER.

260. DREW BREES

261. PEYTON MANNING

262. BRETT FAVRE

263. TOM BRADY

264. DAN MARINO

265. BEN ROETHLISBERGER

266. ELI MANNING

267. PHILIP RIVERS

268. JOHN ELWAY

269. WARREN MOON

270. DAN FOUTS

271. AARON RODGERS

272. JOE MONTANA

273. JOHNNY UNITAS

274. JIM KELLY

275. STEVE YOUNG

276. TROY AIKMAN

277. TERRY BRADSHAW

278. JOE NAMATH

279. ROGER STAUBACH

A. MIAMI (OHIO)

B. MISSISSIPPI

C. MICHIGAN

D. UCLA

E. OKLAHOMA

F. BRIGHAM YOUNG

G. WASHINGTON

H. STANFORD

I. PITTSBURGH

J. NORTH CAROLINA STATE

K. OREGON

L. TENNESSEE

M. PURDUE

N. MIAMI

O. ALABAMA

P. NOTRE DAME

Q. NAVY

R. SOUTHERN MISSISSIPPI

S. LOUISIANA TECH

T. LOUISVILLE

U. CALIFORNIA

BASKETBALL

280. WHO INVENTED THE GAME OF BASKETBALL?
A. PHOG ALLEN
B. RED AUERBACH
C. JAMES NAISMITH
D. DAVID STERN

281. Which NBA player has won the most championships?
a. Bill Russell
b. Kareem Abdul-Jabbar
c. LeBron James
d. Michael Jordan

282. What college did Stephen Curry attend?
a. Davidson
b. Delaware
c. Duke
d. Kentucky

TOUGH TRIVIA CHALLENGE

283. Which of these NBA MVPs has never scored more than 65 points in an NBA game?

a. Kobe Bryant
b. Wilt Chamberlin
c. LeBron James
d. Michael Jordan

284. As of 2018, which NBA player has scored at least 60 points in a game while playing the fewest minutes?

a. Larry Bird
b. James Harden
c. Pete Maravich
d. Klay Thompson

Answers: 260. m; 261. i; 262. r; 263. c; 264. a; 265. a; 266. b; 267. j; 268. h; 269. g; 270. k; 271. u; 272. p; 273. c; 274. n; 275. f; 276. d or e; 277. s; 278. o; 279. q; 280. c; 281. a, with 11; 282. a; 283. c; 284. d

ARE THESE HALL OF FAMERS MEMBERS OF THE NBA'S 20.000 CAREER POINTS CLUB (YES OR NO)?

285. JOHN HAVLICEK
286. KARL MALONE
287. JAMES WORTHY
288. ROBERT PARISH
289. HAKEEM OLAJUWON
290. BERNARD KING
291. GEORGE GERVIN
292. SCOTTIE PIPPEN
293. GRANT HILL
294. WALT FRAZIER
295. ELVIN HAYES
296. STEVE NASH
297. CLYDE DREXLER
298. REGGIE MILLER
299. JOHN STOCKTON
300. BILL RUSSELL

301. DAVID ROBINSON
302. KEVIN MCHALE
303. PETE MARAVICH
304. BOB COUSY
305. ISIAH THOMAS
306. MOSES MALONE
307. JASON KIDD
308. DAVE COWENS
309. RAY ALLEN
310. MAGIC JOHNSON
311. ADRIAN DANTLEY
312. PATRICK EWING
313. TRACY MCGRADY
314. DOMINIQUE WILKINS
315. GARY PAYTON

TOUGH TRIVIA CHALLENGE

316. Which Basketball Hall of Famer was not on the Dream Team in the 1992 Olympics?

a. Charles Barkley
b. Scottie Pippen
c. Chris Mullin
d. Isiah Thomas

317. True or false? Kobe Bryant was drafted by a team other than the Los Angeles Lakers.

▲▲▲▲▲▲▲▲▲▲▲▲▲▲▲▲▲

318. While sitting out the beginning of the 1976 NBA season, Hall of Fame center Dave Cowens briefly worked as a

_____.

a. teacher   c. line cook
b. bank teller   d. cab driver

▲▲▲▲▲▲▲▲▲▲▲▲▲▲▲▲▲▲▲▲▲▲▲

Match the NBA star to the country he was born in.

319. Manu Ginobili
320. Joel Embiid
321. Tony Parker
322. Hakeem Olajuwon
323. Rudy Gobert
324. Al Horford
325. Kyrie Irving
326. Steve Nash
327. Luka Doncic
328. Pau Gasol
329. Giannis Antetokounmpo
330. Patrick Ewing
331. Dirk Nowitzki
332. Luol Deng

a. Argentina
b. Australia
c. Dominican Republic
d. Sudan
e. Germany
f. Belgium
g. Spain
h. Greece
i. Jamaica
j. Nigeria
k. Slovenia
l. South Africa
m. Cameroon
n. France

Answers: 285. yes; 286. yes; 287. no; 288. yes; 289. yes; 290. yes; 291. yes; 292. no; 293. no; 294. no; 295. yes; 296. no; 297. yes; 298. yes; 299. no; 300. no; 301. yes; 302. no; 303. no; 304. no; 305. no; 306. yes; 307. no; 308. no; 309. yes; 310. no; 311. yes; 312. yes; 313. no; 314. yes; 315. yes; 316. d; 317. true, the Charlotte Hornets; 318. d; 319. a; 320. m; 321. n; 322. j; 323. n; 324. c; 325. b; 326. l; 327. k; 328. g; 329. h; 330. i; 331. e; 332. d

Sports & Other Games • **23**

333. As of 2018, who is the only NBA player to lead the NBA in scoring and assists in the same season?

    a. Allen Iverson   c. Joe Fulks

    b. Tiny Archibald   d. James Harden

334. What future U.S. senator was named NCAA player of the year and led Princeton to the final four in 1965?

    a. Bill Bradley

    b. Jerry Lucas

    c. Bill Russell

    d. Bill Walton

335. Over the course of four years, how many games did Diana Taurasi lose while starring for the UConn women's basketball team?

    a. 2   c. 8

    b. 4   d. 16

TOUGH TRIVIA CHALLENGE

336. As of 2018, who is the WNBA's all-time leading scorer?

    a. Candace Parker

    b. Diana Taurasi

    c. Sheryl Swoopes

    d. Sue Bird

337. Cheryl Miller and former UConn star _____ are the only two women to win the Naismith College Basketball Player of the year award three times.

    a. Breanna Stewart

    b. Diana Taurasi

    c. Maya Moore

    d. Sue Bird

MATCH THE PLAYER WITH HIS NICKNAME.

338. Giannis Antetokounmpo
339. Charles Barkley
340. Larry Bird
341. Kobe Bryant
342. Wilt Chamberlain
343. Clyde Drexler
344. Tim Duncan
345. Julius Erving
346. Walt Frazier
347. Kevin Garnett
348. George Gervin
349. Anfernee Hardaway
350. John Havlicek
351. Allen Iverson
352. LeBron James
353. Karl Malone
354. Pete Maravich
355. Hakeem Olajuwon
356. Robert Parish
357. Gary Payton
358. Paul Pierce
359. Oscar Robertson
360. David Robinson
361. Jerry West
362. Dominique Wilkins

a. The Glove
b. The Chief
c. The Logo
d. Clyde
e. The Truth
f. The Round Mound of Rebound
g. The Answer
h. Hondo
i. The Big Fundamental
j. Greek Freak
k. The Legend
l. The Black Mamba
m. The Big Dipper
n. The Glide
o. The Admiral
p. Mailman
q. The Big Ticket
r. The Human Highlight Reel
s. King
t. The Dream
u. Big O
v. The Iceman
w. Dr. J
x. Pistol
y. Penny

363. WHO HOLDS THE NBA RECORD FOR MOST BLOCKS IN A SEASON?

365. NAME THE THREE NON-CENTERS WHO HAVE WON TWO DEFENSIVE PLAYER OF THE YEAR AWARDS.

TOUGH TRIVIA CHALLENGE

364. Who are the two men who have won four Defensive Player of the Year awards?

As of 2018, had these NBA MVPs ever been named to an NBA All-Defense Team (yes or no)?

366. Michael Jordan
367. Larry Bird
368. Allen Iverson
369. Bill Russell
370. Steve Nash
371. Dirk Nowitzki
372. Russell Westbrook

373. Tim Duncan
374. Kevin Garnett
375. Charles Barkley
376. Magic Johnson

377. What franchise has won the most NBA titles?

378. True or false? No player has ever won an NBA scoring title while playing for the Boston Celtics.

379. What center won the 1977-78 NBA MVP despite only playing in 58 games?

380. WHICH LEGEND LOST MORE GAMES IN THEIR UCLA CAREER, KAREEM ABDUL-JABBAR OR BILL WALTON?

381. Who is the shortest player to be named **NBA MVP?**

382. As of 2018, who are the only two men that have won a Sixth Man of the Year award and are in the Hall of Fame?

383. True or false? Kobe Bryant was twice named Most Outstanding Player in the NCAA Final Four.

Match the college alma mater to the NBA All-Star.

384. Auburn	a. Kareem Abdul-Jabbar
385. California	b. Ray Allen
386. Central Arkansas	c. Carmelo Anthony
387. Cincinnati	d. Charles Barkley
388. Connecticut	e. Larry Bird
389. Georgetown	f. Wilt Chamberlain
390. Gonzaga	g. Tim Duncan
391. Houston	h. Kevin Durant
392. Indiana	i. Blake Griffin
393. Indiana State	j. Allen Iverson
394. Kansas	k. Magic Johnson
395. Kentucky	l. Michael Jordan
396. Louisiana State	m. Jason Kidd
397. Louisiana Tech	n. Karl Malone
398. Marquette	o. Steve Nash
399. Memphis	p. Hakeem Olajuwon
400. Michigan State	q. Shaquille O'Neal
401. Navy	r. Scottie Pippen
402. North Carolina	s. Oscar Robertson
403. Oklahoma	t. David Robinson
404. San Francisco	u. Rajon Rondo
405. Santa Clara	v. Derrick Rose
406. Syracuse	w. Bill Russell
407. Texas	x. John Stockton
408. UCLA	y. Isiah Thomas
409. Wake Forest	z. Dwyane Wade

410. Which college has won the most NCAA men's basketball championships?

    a. Duke

    b. Kentucky

    c. North Carolina

    d. UCLA

TOUGH TRIVIA CHALLENGE

412. Which coach has won the most NCAA basketball championships?
a. Geno Auriemma
b. Mike Krzyzewski
c. Pat Summitt
d. John Wooden

411. WHICH COLLEGE HAS WON THE MOST NCAA WOMEN'S BASKETBALL CHAMPIONSHIPS, UCONN OR TENNESSEE?

Answers: 384. d; 385. m; 386. r; 387. s; 388. b; 389. j; 390. x; 391. p; 392. y; 393. z; 394. f; 395. u; 396. q; 397. n; 398. z; 399. v; 400. k; 401. t; 402. l; 403. i; 404. i; 405. o; 406. c; 407. h; 408. a; 409. g; 410. d, with 11; 411. UConn, with 11; 412. a, with 11

413. How many minutes is a fighting penalty?

414. **True or false?** If you took away all of Wayne Gretzky's goals, he would still be the NHL's all-time leading scorer as of 2018.

415. **As of 2018, who has scored the most goals in NHL history?**
   a. Alex Ovechkin
   b. Gordie Howe
   c. Mario Lemieux
   d. Wayne Gretzky

416. Which was not one of the "Original Six" NHL franchises?

   a. Boston Bruins
   b. Montreal Canadiens
   c. Philadelphia Flyers
   d. Toronto Maple Leafs

TOUGH TRIVIA CHALLENGE

417. As of 2018, who is the only defenseman to lead the NHL in scoring for a season?
   a. Bobby Orr
   b. Chris Pronger
   c. Nicklas Lidstrom
   d. Paul Coffey

418. **True or False?** No NHL player has ever averaged more than a goal a game (min. 50 goals).

MATCH THE NHL AWARD TO THE ACHIEVEMENT IT HONORS.

419. Jack Adams Trophy
420. Lady Byng Trophy
421. Calder Trophy
422. Hart Memorial Trophy
423. William M. Jennings Trophy
424. James Norris Memorial Trophy
425. Presidents' Trophy
426. Maurice "Rocket" Richard Trophy
427. Art Ross Trophy
428. Conn Smythe Trophy
429. Vezina Trophy

a. Best combination of skill and sportsmanship
b. Best defenseman
c. Best goalie
d. Coach of the Year
e. Fewest goals allowed
f. Most goals scored
g. Most points, regular season (team)
h. Most points, regular season (player)
i. Most Valuable Player (regular season)
j. Most Valuable Player (Stanley Cup playoffs)
k. Rookie of the Year

430. Who is the only individual to win the Stanley Cup as a player and an owner?

a. Wayne Gretzky
b. Mario Lemieux
c. Bobby Orr
d. Maurice Richard

431. WHY WAS THERE NO WINNER OF THE 1919 STANLEY CUP?

A. FLU EPIDEMIC
B. PLAYER STRIKE
C. WORLD WAR I
D. THE CUP DIDN'T EXIST UNTIL 1920

Answers: 413. five; 414. true; 415. d; 416. c; 417. a; 418. false; Wayne Gretzky, Mario Lemieux, Brett Hull, and Cam Neely have done it; 419. d; 420. a; 421. k; 422. i; 423. e; 424. b; 425. g; 426. f; 427. h; 428. j; 429. c; 430. b; 431. a.

Sports & Other Games • 37

SOCCER

432. As of 2018, who has scored the most goals in Champions League play?
a. Pelé
b. Lionel Messi
c. Diego Maradona
d. Cristiano Ronaldo

433. As of 2018, who has scored the most goals in men's World Cup play?
a. Pelé
b. Thierry Henry
c. Miroslav Klose
d. Cristiano Ronaldo

434. Where was the first men's World Cup held?
a. Brazil   c. Argentina
b. Uruguay d. Colombia

435. What is the only country to have played in every men's World Cup?
a. Italy   c. Brazil
b. England d. Germany

436. What country has won the most men's World Cup titles?
a. Italy   c. Brazil
b. France d. Germany

437. What is Pelé's real name?
a. Edson
b. João
c. Manu
d. Tiago

438. Who has scored more goals in the women's World Cup, Brazil's Marta or the United States' Abby Wambach?

439. What country has won the most women's World Cup titles?

a. Brazil   c. Japan

b. Germany   d. United States

440. WHAT COUNTRY WON THE FIRST WOMEN'S WORLD CUP?

BOXING

441. Which is heavier: A lightweight boxer or a bantamweight boxer?

443. WHO FOUGHT IN THE "THRILLA IN MANILA"?

TOUGH TRIVIA CHALLENGE

442. In 1994, George Foreman became the oldest heavyweight champion ever at what age?

a. 36   c. 42

b. 39   d. 45

444. Who is the only heavyweight champion to retire undefeated?

    a. Muhammad Ali   c. Rocky Marciano

    b. Mike Tyson   d. Joe Louis

445. Who was the first boxer to win championships at five different weight classes?

a. Thomas Hearns   c. Manny Pacquiao

b. Floyd Mayweather Jr.   d. Sugar Ray Robinson

MATCH THE NICKNAME TO THE BOXER.

446. THE MANASSA MAULER
447. THE BROCKTON BLOCKBUSTER
448. HURRICANE
449. THE GREATEST
450. SMOKIN' JOE
451. THE RAGING BULL

A. MUHAMMAD ALI
B. RUBIN CARTER
C. JACK DEMPSEY
D. JOE FRAZIER
E. JAKE LAMOTTA
F. ROCKY MARCIANO

GOLF

452. How many clubs is a player allowed to carry in a round of golf?

453. Which famous Scottish course is believed to be the first in the world?

454. Who holds the record for largest margin of victory in a major?

    a. Rory McIlroy

    b. Jack Nicklaus

    c. Tiger Woods

    d. Ben Hogan

TOUGH TRIVIA CHALLENGE

455. As of 2018, who has the most official victories on the PGA Tour?

    a. Tiger Woods

    b. Sam Snead

    c. Jack Nicklaus

    d. Byron Nelson

456. Who holds the record for most wins in a single season on the PGA Tour?

    a. Byron Nelson   **c. Sam Snead**

    b. Jack Nicklaus   **d. Tiger Woods**

457. Who is the last amateur to win a tournament on the PGA Tour?

    a. Phil Mickelson   c. David Duval

    b. Tiger Woods   d. Trip Kuehne

458. What legendary American author said that golf "is a good walk spoiled"?

    a. William Faulkner   c. Ernest Hemingway

    b. Herman Melville   d. Mark Twain

MISCELLANEOUS

459. WHICH TENNIS GREAT WON SIX STRAIGHT WIMBLEDON SINGLES TITLES IN THE 1980S?

    A. BJORN BORG   C. JOHN MCENROE

    B. STEFFI GRAF   D. MARTINA NAVRATILOVA

460. True or false? Like the Olympics and World Cup, the Tour de France is held once every four years.

461. HOW MANY RINGS ARE THERE ON THE OLYMPIC FLAG?

Answers: 446. c; 447. f; 448. b; 449. a; 450. d; 451. e; 452. 14; 453. the Old Course at St. Andrews; 454. c, 15 strokes at the 2000 U.S. Open; 455. b, with 82; 456. d, with 18 in 1945; 457. a; 458. d; 459. d; 460. false; 461. five

Sports & Other Games • 35

Match the college to its nickname.

462. Georgetown	a. Tar Heels
463. Maryland	b. Fighting Irish
464. Texas	c. Sooners
465. Notre Dame	d. Longhorns
466. Minnesota	e. Blue Devils
467. Wisconsin	f. Bruins
468. Clemson	g. Orange
469. Texas A&M	h. Terrapins
470. Alabama	i. Ducks
471. Duke	j. Boilermakers
472. Stanford	k. Crimson Tide
473. Indiana	l. Bulldogs
474. Purdue	m. Wolverines
475. UCLA	n. Badgers
476. Michigan	o. Hoyas
477. Vanderbilt	p. Tigers
478. Wake Forest	q. Demon Deacons
479. Arizona State	r. Hurricanes
480. Oklahoma	s. Cavaliers
481. Syracuse	t. Cardinal
482. Oregon	u. Sun Devils
483. Nebraska	v. Hoosiers
484. Virginia	w. Golden Gophers
485. Georgia	x. Cornhuskers
486. North Carolina	y. Aggies
487. Miami	z. Commodores

Match the movie to the sport it is centered around.

488. *Rudy*
489. *Miracle*
490. *The Bad News Bears*
491. *Chariots of Fire*
492. *Breaking Away*
493. *Hoosiers*

a. cycling
b. track
c. football
d. basketball
e. hockey
f. baseball

· GAMES ·

494. On early Egyptian playing cards, which of these was not a symbol?
a. cups   c. swords
b. coins   d. crowns

495. Which county added the joker to the playing card deck?

a. England   c. Italy
b. Germany   d. United States

496. WHAT IS THE NAME OF THE QUEEN IN CANDY LAND?

Answers: 462. o; 463. h; 464. d; 465. b; 466. w; 467. n; 468. p; 469. y; 470. k; 471. e; 472. t; 473. v; 474. j; 475. f; 476. m; 477. z; 478. q; 479. u; 480. c; 481. g; 482. i; 483. x; 484. s; 485. l; 486. a; 487. r; 488. c; 489. e; 490. f; 491. b; 492. a; 493. d; 494. d; 495. d. 496. Queen Frostine

Sports & Other Games · **37**

497. Before the name was changed in 2002, what was the Chocolate Swamp in Candy Land known as?

a. Caramel Cove
b. Molasses Swamp
c. Peanut Butter Pond
d. Skittles Swamp

498. In Clue, what is the name of the Colonel?

499. What is Mr. Green known as in the British edition of Clue?

a. Parson Green
b. Rev. Green
c. Monsieur Green
d. Sen. Green

500. Which of the following is not a room in Clue?

a. Study
b. Conservatory
c. Bar
d. Library

501. What player always goes first in a game of Clue?

502. IN OTHELLO. WHO MAKES THE FIRST MOVE. LIGHT OR DARK?

503. True or false? According to the rules of Monopoly, you collect money from the center of the board when you land on Free Parking.

504. What are the first two purchasable properties on the Monopoly board?

505. WHAT ARE THE FOUR RAILROADS IN MONOPOLY?

506. What is the only street in Monopoly that is not located in Atlantic City, New Jersey?

507. Does a Monopoly game contain more or less than $15,000 in play money?

508. What is the name of the individual in the Monopoly Jail?
   a. David the Deceptive
   b. Fred the Fraudulent
   c. Jake the Jailbird
   d. Peter the Prisoner

TOUGH TRIVIA CHALLENGE

509. How many properties are there in Monopoly?
   a. 24   c. 28
   b. 26   d. 30

510. Other than Jail, what is the most commonly landed upon Monopoly square?
a. Go   c. Illinois Avenue
b. New York Avenue   d. B&O Railroad

511. What was Mr. Monopoly's name before it was changed in 1999?

512. How much money does each player start with in a game of Monopoly?
   a. $500   c. $1500
   b. $1000   d. $2000

513. TRUE OR FALSE? MONOPOLY WAS BANNED IN THE COMMUNIST SOVIET UNION.

514. WHAT PROPERTY COMPLETES THE MONOPOLY IF YOU OWN ST. CHARLES PLACE AND VIRGINIA AVENUE?

515. What property completes the monopoly if you own Marvin Gardens and Atlantic Avenue?

516. What property completes the monopoly if you own Oriental Avenue and Connecticut Avenue?

517. What property completes the monopoly if you own Pennsylvania Avenue and North Carolina Avenue?

518. What property completes the monopoly if you own New York Avenue and Tennessee Avenue?

519. What property completes the monopoly if you own Indiana Avenue and Illinois Avenue?

520. When did the New York Times begin publishing crossword puzzles?

    a. 1936   c. 1942

    b. 1939   d. 1948

TOUGH TRIVIA CHALLENGE

521. What is the term for a person who is skillful at creating crossword puzzles?

  a. crucifixitionist c. cruciverbalist

  b. crucibler   d. rosicrucian

522. When did the Pokémon trading card game first enter the Japanese market?

    a. 1976 c. 1996

    b. 1986 d. 2001

523. How many cards do you draw at the beginning of a basic game of Pokémon?

524. In Risk, what continent has the most territories?

525. IF TWO PLAYERS ARE PLAYING RISK, HOW MANY ARMIES DOES EACH PLAYER START WITH?

    A. 30 C. 50

    B. 40 D. 60

526. In Risk, what is the minimum number of armies you need to have in a country in order to attack a neighboring country?

    a. 1   c. 4

    b. 2   d. 8

527. Which of the following are not a territory in Risk?

a. Venezuela c. Italy

b. Quebec   d. Japan

528. How many A tiles are there in a game of Scrabble?

    a. 3   c. 9

    b. 6   d. 12

529. How many points is an M worth in a game of Scrabble?

    a. 2   **c. 4**

    b. 3   **d. 5**

◆ ◆ ◆ ◆ ◆ ◆ ◆ ◆ ◆ ◆ ◆ ◆ ◆

530. Which of the following words is impossible to get in Scrabble without using a blank tile?

    a. quagmire   c. pizza

    b. quixotic   d. albatross

◆ ◆ ◆ ◆ ◆ ◆ ◆ ◆ ◆ ◆ ◆ ◆ ◆

531. True or false? **Alfred Butts, the individual who created Scrabble, also created Boggle.**

◆ ◆ ◆ ◆ ◆ ◆ ◆ ◆ ◆ ◆ ◆ ◆ ◆

532. The individual who created Scrabble also created a game called _____.

    a. Alfred's Other Game

    b. Al Aboard

    c. Call Me Al

    d. Al the Pal

533. How many spaces wide is a Scrabble board?

    a. 12   c. 18

    b. 15   d. 21

◆ ◆ ◆ ◆ ◆ ◆ ◆ ◆ ◆ ◆ ◆ ◆ ◆ ◆

534. Are there more P tiles or U tiles in Scrabble?

TOUGH TRIVIA CHALLENGE

535. In the 1960s version of the Game of Life, you could end up at the _____.

a. Poor Farm

b. Retirement Home

c. Town Dump

d. White House

536. What two numbers, between 1 and 12, are not featured on the cards in a game of Sorry!?

    a. 2 and 4   c. 6 and 9

    b. 3 and 6   d. 7 and 8

Match the Trivial Pursuit category with its associated color.

537. Geography
538. Entertainment
539. Arts & Literature
540. Science & Nature
541. Sports & Leisure
542. History

a. pink
b. blue
c. green
d. orange
e. brown
f. yellow

◆ ◆ ◆ ◆ ◆ ◆ ◆ ◆ ◆ ◆ ◆ ◆ ◆ ◆ ◆ ◆ ◆

545. What is another common term for dominoes?

a. tiles   c. bones
b. tuxedoes   d. penguins

◆ ◆ ◆ ◆ ◆ ◆ ◆ ◆ ◆ ◆ ◆ ◆ ◆ ◆ ◆ ◆ ◆

546. How is a player eliminated in Settlers of Catan?

◆ ◆ ◆ ◆ ◆ ◆ ◆ ◆ ◆ ◆ ◆ ◆ ◆ ◆ ◆ ◆

547. Which of the following is not a resource in the basic Settlers of Catan game?

a. brick   c. grain
b. lumber   d. gold

TOUGH TRIVIA CHALLENGE

543. The odds of rolling five of a kind on your first Yahtzee roll is

_____.

a. 1 in 522
b. 1 in 1296
c. 1 in 2500
d. 1 in 3725

544. HOW MANY TILES IN A STANDARD SET OF DOMINOES?

A. 24
B. 28
C. 32
D. 36

◆ ◆ ◆ ◆ ◆ ◆ ◆ ◆ ◆ ◆ ◆ ◆ ◆ ◆ ◆

548. WHAT IS THE HIGHEST HAND IN POKER (WITH NO WILD CARDS)?

549. How many players can play Chinese Checkers at one time?

550. When was Dungeons & Dragons first released?
a. 1968
c. 1979
b. 1974
d. 1987

551. Which of the following is not a part of your character's Dungeons & Dragons ability score?

a. Strength
c. Wisdom
b. Fortitude
d. Charisma

552. What is an NPC in Dungeons & Dragons?

553. Which of the following was not a player class in the first edition of Dungeons & Dragons?

a. Monk
c. Cleric
b. Bard
d. Leader

554. What alignment in Dungeons & Dragons is the opposite of Lawful-Good?

555. Which of the following bands reference Dungeons & Dragons in a song?
a. Guns N' Roses
b. Led Zeppelin
c. Weezer
d. LCD Soundsystem

556. What is the title of the Rona Jaffe novel where a troubled college student becomes dangerously obsessed with a Dungeons & Dragons-type game?
a. *Lizards and Labyrinths*
b. *Mazes and Monsters*
c. *Treasures and Trolls*
d. *Witches and Warriors*

557. A character's ability to withstand further attack in Dungeons & Dragons is measured in what?
a. Damage Points
b. Hit Points
c. Life Points
d. Vita Points

Answers: 537, b; 538, a; 539, e; 540, c; 541, d; 542, f; 543, b; 544, b; 545, c; 546, they cannot be eliminated; 547, d; 548, royal flush; 549, 6; 550, b; 551, b; 552, Non-Player Character; 553, d; 554, Chaotic-Evil; 555, c; 556, c; 557, b.

Sports & Other Games • **43**

558. What was the first home video game system?

 a. Atari 2600
 b. Magnavox Odyssey
 c. Nintendo Entertainment System
 d. Sega Genesis

559. The Nintendo Entertainment System was first known as _ _ _ _ _ _ _.

 a. Famicom
 b. Gamicom
 c. Playcom
 d. Zoomcom

560. More than _____ in quarters had been spent on Pac-Man arcade games by 2000.

 a. $125 million
 b. $500 million
 c. $890 million
 d. $2.5 billion

561. What is the name of the predominant land in the universe where the Legend of Zelda takes place?

a. Lorule b. Hyrule
c. Norule d. Tlon

562. What is the name of the villain in the Legend of Zelda?

563. What is the name of the addictive game developed by Russian programmer Alex Pajitnov in 1985?

a. Laika
b. Monopoly
c. Sputnik
d. Tetris

TOUGH TRIVIA CHALLENGE

564. FOR WHAT COMPUTER WAS THE FIRST JOHN MADDEN FOOTBALL GAME DESIGNED?

Answers: 558. b; 559. a; 560. d; 561. b; 562. Ganon; 563. d; 564. Apple II

CHAPTER 2

Scientific Knowledge

ANIMALS

565. Crocodiles, alligators, and caimans are part of this group of reptiles.
   a. crocodilians
   b. alligatians
   c. crocozoids
   d. alligoids

566. True or false? In some reptiles, the temperature of the embryos determines if it will be a boy or girl.

567. True or false? Reptiles have spines.

568. Is a reptile cold-blooded or warm-blooded?

569. ARE MAMMALS WARM-BLOODED OR COLD-BLOODED?

570. Snakes shed their skin _____.

  a. every few days
  b. every few weeks
  c. every few months
  d. every few years

571. What's faster, the fastest reptile or the fastest snake?

572. True or false? Pythons can "see" heat from warm-blooded animals.

573. The tuatara, the closest thing to a dinosaur that's still alive, is a reptile that lives in _ _ _ _ _ _.

  a. New Zealand
  b. New South Wales
  c. New York
  d. New England

TOUGH TRIVIA CHALLENGE

574. On a tortoise, which is the top shell, the carapace or the plastron?

575. What egg-laying mammal also has a poison-tipped spur behind each leg?

MATCH THE ANIMAL
TO THE NAME FOR ITS DWELLING.

576. eagle
577. bear
578. rabbit
579. beaver
580. penguin
581. pig

a. lodge
b. warren
d. rookery
e. den
f. aerie
g. sty

582. True or false? An African buffalo's horns help it float in water.

583. IT IS POSSIBLE TO DETERMINE THE AGE OF AN AMERICAN BISON BY LOOKING AT THE SHAPE OF ITS _____.

A. EYES
B. FACE
C. HORNS
D. TAIL

584. HOW MANY TOES DOES A BLACK BEAR HAVE ON EACH PAW?

585. What color is a polar bear's skin?

586. What is a faster swimmer, a killer whale or a dolphin?

587. True or false? A dolphin sleeps with one eye open.

588. True or false? The eye of an ostrich is larger than its brain.

589. Koalas and wallabies are diprotodonts. What does that mean?

a. their feet and hands are different shapes

b. they are marsupials with two incisors in their lower jaw

c. they eat eucalyptus

d. they have two stomachs

590. True or false? Koalas have two thumbs on each of their hands.

591. True or false? All zebras have the same stripe pattern.

592. The tongue of an adult giant anteater is approximately _____ on average.

a. 9 inches long

b. 15 inches long

c. 24 inches long

d. 36 inches long

593. How many vertebrae are in a giraffe's neck?
a. 7
b. 17
c. 70
d. 700

594. DO GIRAFFES HAVE EYELASHES?

595. The giant panda's false thumb is actually a _____.
   a. chunk of fatty tissue
   b. large wrist bone
   c. excess skin
   d. claw

596. True or false? A hedgehog's spine is hollow.

597. TRUE OR FALSE? A HYENA'S STOMACH CAN DIGEST BONES.

598. ARE MOST MONGOOSE SPECIES HERBIVORES, CARNIVORES, OR OMNIVORES?

599. True or false? A red kangaroo can run as fast as 40 mph.

600. The lion is the second-largest cat. What's the first?

601. Which is larger, the Sumatran rhino or the Indian rhino?

♦ ♦ ♦ ♦ ♦ ♦ ♦ ♦ ♦ ♦ ♦ ♦ ♦ ♦ ♦ ♦

602. Which has more horns, the Sumatran rhino or the Indian rhino?

♦ ♦

603. Is a Tasmanian devil a marsupial or a rodent?

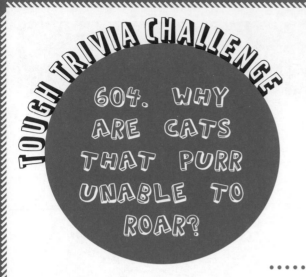

604. WHY ARE CATS THAT PURR UNABLE TO ROAR?

608. The cheetah is the fastest carnivore on Earth. What is the fastest herbivore?
- a. black bear
- b. kangaroo
- c. North American pronghorn
- d. zebra

605. Where are a cricket's ears located?
- a. front legs
- b. hind legs
- c. sides of head
- d. wings

609. Musk is widely considered the most powerful scent in the world. Is it produced by the male or female musk deer?

606. Does a wolf have more teeth on its upper jaw or its lower jaw?

610. What is the smaller species of camelidae, the llama or the vicuna?

607. When hand-milked, approximately how many squirts does it take for a cow to produce a gallon of milk?
- a. 85
- b. 125
- c. 235
- d. 345

611. On average, how many quills does a porcupine have?

    a. 300
    b. 1,500
    c. 15,000
    d. 30,000

612. True or false? Spiders are part of an animal group called arthropods, a group that also includes shrimp.

673. TRUE OR FALSE? ALL SPIDERS SPIN WEBS.

614. TRUE OR FALSE? SOME SPIDERS USE THEIR SILK TO FISH.

615. True or false? Spiders eat their extra silk.

616. Spiders are oviparous. What does that mean?

    a. they emit noxious odors
    b. their babies develop in eggs
    c. they have eight legs
    d. they can release poison

617. True or false? Dogs have sweat glands between their paws.

618. WHAT COLOR ARE ALL DALMATIANS BORN?

619. True or false? The Basenji is the only dog breed that doesn't bark.

620. Which tend to live longer, dogs with flat faces or dogs with long faces?

621. True or false? Each African wild dog has a different pattern in its coat.

622. The U.S. has the highest population of dogs. What country has the second highest?
   a. Canada
   b. China
   c. France
   d. Germany

623. Which came first, fish or dinosaurs?

624. True or false? There is no fish than can crawl outside of water or absorb oxygen.

MATCH THE UNPLEASANT NAME TO THE NICER, NEWER NAME.

625. Slimeheads

626. Rock crabs

627. Pilchards

628. Patagonian toothfish

a. Peekytoe crabs

b. Chilean seabass

c. Orange Roughy

d. Cornish sardines

629. The size difference between the smallest shark (the spined pygmy) and the largest (the whale shark) is approximately _____.
   a. 28 feet
   b. 35 feet
   c. 42 feet
   d. 49 feet

630. True or false? Baby great white sharks are nurtured by their mothers for up to six months.

631. WHAT IS A BABY SHARK CALLED?

632. TRUE OR FALSE? AFTER EATING A SEA MAMMAL SUCH AS A SEA LION, A SHARK CAN SOMETIMES GO TWO MONTHS WITHOUT ANOTHER MAJOR MEAL.

633. Is it male or female mosquitoes that bite?

_ _ _ _ _ _ _

634. According to the American Kennel Club, what is the most popular dog breed in the U.S.?
a. Golden Retriever
b. Labrador Retriever
c. German Shepherd
d. Pit Bull Terrier

_ _ _ _ _ _ _

636. What food makes up around 99 percent of a giant panda's diet?

_ _ _ _ _ _ _

637. True or false? Mice live for 10 years on average.

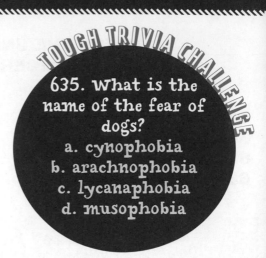

TOUGH TRIVIA CHALLENGE

635. What is the name of the fear of dogs?
a. cynophobia
b. arachnophobia
c. lycanaphobia
d. musophobia

638. Why do crocodiles frequently sleep with their mouths open?

a. to catch prey

b. to keep from snoring

c. to clean their teeth

d. to release heat

_ _ _ _ _ _ _

639. What are female elephants called?

_ _ _ _ _ _ _

640. A mule is a cross between a female horse and a male _ _ _ _ _ _.

641. Approximately how deep is the Earth's crust?

    a. 10 miles   b. 15 miles

    c. 25 miles   d. 30 miles

642. True or false? The Earth's inner core is estimated to be about the size of the Moon.

644. Which period in the Earth's history came first, the Priscoan or the Archean?

645. Which came first, the Jurassic Period or the Cretaceous Period?

TOUGH TRIVIA CHALLENGE

643. Approximately how much shorter are mountains estimated to get every 1,000 years?
a. 3 inches
b. 3 feet
c. 30 feet
d. 300 feet

646. True or false? Dinosaur fossils have been found on every continent on Earth.

647. True or false? Scientists have calculated that the Earth reverses its polarity every 200,000 years.

◆ ◆ ◆ ◆ ◆ ◆ ◆ ◆ ◆ ◆ ◆ ◆ ◆ ◆ ◆

648. Does the Earth contain more aluminum or potassium?

◆ ◆ ◆ ◆ ◆ ◆ ◆ ◆ ◆ ◆ ◆ ◆ ◆ ◆ ◆

649. What percentage of the Earth is covered by water?
a. 46%   b. 57%
c. 71%   d. 85%

◆ ◆ ◆ ◆ ◆ ◆ ◆ ◆ ◆ ◆ ◆ ◆ ◆ ◆ ◆

650. Approximately what percent of the Earth's land area is covered in ice?

a. 2%
b. 5%
c. 10%
d. 20%

651. WHAT IS THE ONLY CONTINENT WITHOUT MOUNTAIN GLACIERS?

◆ ◆ ◆ ◆ ◆ ◆ ◆ ◆ ◆ ◆ ◆ ◆ ◆ ◆ ◆

652. Approximately how much of an iceberg is typically above the water level?
a. 10 percent b. 20 percent
c. 30 percent d. 50 percent

◆ ◆ ◆ ◆ ◆ ◆ ◆ ◆ ◆ ◆ ◆ ◆ ◆ ◆ ◆

653. In the open sea, approximately how deep can sunlight reach underwater in normal conditions?
a. 250 feet   b. 450 feet
c. 650 feet   d. 850 feet

654. Which is deeper, the Atlantic or the Pacific?

◆◆◆◆◆◆◆◆◆◆◆◆◆◆◆◆

655. What is the average salt content of the world's oceans?
a. 1 percent
b. 2.2 percent
c. 3.5 percent
d. 4.8 percent

◆◆◆◆◆◆◆◆◆◆◆◆◆◆◆◆

656. What is the name of the deepest point in the world's oceans?
a. Grand Canyon
b. Mariana Trench
c. Zissou Trench
d. Cameron Abyss

◆◆◆◆◆◆◆◆◆◆◆◆◆◆◆◆

657. A hotter and dryer climate means that the salt content in a nearby ocean will be lower or higher?

TOUGH TRIVIA CHALLENGE

658. Where are the strongest tidal currents found?
a. Florida's Atlantic coast
b. Chile
c. Antarctica
d. Finland

659. Which weather pattern features warmer ocean water, El Niño or La Niña?

◆◆◆◆◆◆◆◆◆◆◆◆◆◆

660. Hurricanes form in the Atlantic. What name is given to a similar storm in the Pacific?

◆◆◆◆◆◆◆◆◆◆◆◆◆◆

661. True or false? Sound travels faster through water than through air.

Answers: 647: true; 648: potassium; 649: c; 650: c; 651: Australia; 652: a; 653: c; 654: Pacific; 655: c; 656: b; 657: higher; 658: d; 659: El Niño; 660: typhoon; 661: true

Scientific Knowledge • **61**

662. What is another name for a tidal wave?

663. What is the name of the weather instrument used to measure atmospheric pressure?

664. High atmospheric pressure will result in _.
a. clear blue skies
b. thunderstorms
c. clouds
d. rain showers

665. Nimbus, cumulus, and stratus are examples of what?

666. What type of cloud appears as a blanket of clouds in the sky?

667. WHAT TYPE OF CLOUD CAN BE DESCRIBED AS WISPY AND THIN?

668. What continent holds the record for hottest temperature ever recorded?
a. Africa
b. Australia
c. North America
d. South America

669. What is the calm area at the center of the hurricane called?
a. the core
b. the heart
c. the middle
d. the eye

670. In the United States, weather patterns mostly move from _____.

a. East to West
b. West to East
c. North to South
d. South to North

671. What is between the Earth's stratosphere and the mesosphere?

672. According to NASA, approximately how thick is the Earth's atmosphere?

a. 15 miles
b. 30 miles
c. 45 miles
d. 60 miles

673. True or false? Small earthquakes happen every day on Earth.

674. What is the name of the scale used to measure the magnitude of earthquakes?

675. How much more powerful is a 6.0 than a 5.0 on the Richter scale?

a. 1x
b. 5x
c. 10x
d. 100x

Answers: 662. tsunami; 663. a barometer; 664. a; 665. clouds; 666. stratus; 667. cirrus; 668. c, 134.1°F at Furnace Creek, CA in 1913; 669. d; 670. b; 671. the ozone layer; 672. d; 673. true; 674. Richter scale; 675. c

Scientific Knowledge • **63**

676. Where was the strongest earthquake ever recorded?
a. Philippines
b. Chile
c. Kenya
d. China

HOW ABOUT 9.7 ON THE PANIC SCALE?

677. THE *LOCATION* WHERE THE EARTH FIRST MOVES *IN* AN EARTHQUAKE *IS* CALLED WHAT?

678. What U.S. National Park has a 37-mile-long chamber of magma underneath it?
a. Acadia
b. Glacier
c. Yellowstone
d. Yosemite

679. When lava cools, which type of rock is formed?
a. sedimentary
b. igneous
c. metamorphic
d. none of the above

··PLANTS··

680. TRUE OR FALSE? THE OLDEST LIVING TREE, A BRISTLECONE PINE, IS OVER 5,000 YEARS OLD.

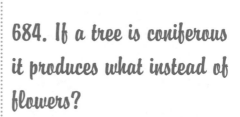

681. Where is the world's oldest tree located?

682. The first Arbor Day was celebrated in what year?
- a. 1776
- b. 1872
- c. 1914
- d. 1967

683. What causes a tree to be classified as deciduous?
- a. produces sap
- b. loses all its leaves and needles in a year
- c. lives for 10 years
- d. produces single-colored leaves

684. If a tree is coniferous it produces what instead of flowers?

685. True or false? A wild fig tree in South Africa has roots going down 400 feet.

686. The state tree of New York, Wisconsin, Vermont, and West Virginia has the Latin name Acer saccharin. What is it better known as?

a. Sugar Maple
b. Elm
c. Douglas Fir
d. Tulip Poplar

687. Approximately how much CO2 does a large tree clean from the atmosphere each year?

a. 70 pounds
b. 110 pounds
c. 220 pounds
d. 330 pounds

688. True or false? No wild plant produces a black flower.

689. Which came first: flowering plants or ferns?

690. WHAT IS FOSSILIZED TREE RESIN CALLED?

691. Which part of a plant produces most of its food?

a. leaves   b. stem

c. roots   d. flowers

---

692. There are approximately 80,000 plant species in the world that are edible for humans. Approximately how many are actively cultivated for food?

     a. 25   b. 150

     c. 480   d. 900

---

693. True or false? In the right conditions bamboo can grow over 2 feet in one day.

---

694. A climbing plant is also known as a _____.

TOUGH TRIVIA CHALLENGE

695. Saffron is the most expensive spice on Earth, with high-quality offerings costing almost $5,000 USD a pound. Approximately how many flowers are needed to produce one pound?

a. 25,000

b. 50,000

c. 75,000

d. 100,000

---

696. True or false? Apple seeds contain the poison cyanide.

---

697. What is pomology?

---

698. What is the study of fungi known as?

a. ecology

b. fungology

c. mycology

d. morphology

Answers: 686. a; 687. d; 688. true; 689. ferns; 690. amber; 691. a; 692. b; 693. true; 694. vine; 695. c; 696. true; 697. the study of fruits; 698. c.

Scientific Knowledge • **67**

• SPACE IS THE PLACE •

699. What element makes up approximately 75 percent of the sun?

▲▲▲▲▲▲▲▲▲▲▲▲▲▲▲

700. What is the second most common element in the sun's composition?

a. carbon
b. helium
c. nitrogen
d. oxygen

▲▲▲▲▲▲▲▲▲▲▲▲▲▲▲

701. Approximately how hot is the surface of the sun?

a. 10,000°F
b. 50,000°F
c. 100,000°F
d. 1,000,000°F

TOUGH TRIVIA CHALLENGE

702. Approximately how old is the sun's light by the time it reaches the Earth?
a. 8 seconds
b. 8 minutes
c. 8 days
d. 8 years

703. True or false? The sun holds more than 99 percent of our solar system's mass.

▲▲▲▲▲▲▲▲▲▲▲▲▲▲

704. What type of galaxy is the most common in the universe: elliptical, irregular, or spiral?

705. What is the name of a star that has exhausted its core hydrogen and is now fusing hydrogen outside the core?

▲▲▲▲▲▲▲▲▲▲▲▲▲▲▲

706. Which is smaller, Mercury or Venus?

▲▲▲▲▲▲▲▲▲▲▲▲▲▲▲

707. Saturn, Jupiter, Uranus, and _____ all have rings around them.

▲▲▲▲▲▲▲▲▲▲▲▲▲▲▲

708. True or false? No human has ever been in space for more than 1 year continuously.

▲▲▲▲▲▲▲▲▲▲▲▲▲▲▲

709. ARE THERE MORE OR LESS THAN 100 MOONS IN OUR SOLAR SYSTEM?

710. How many moons does Jupiter have?

a. 57   b. 67

c. 77   d. 87

711. Approximately how many Earth years long is 1 year on Jupiter?

a. 3
b. 5
c. 9
d. 12

712. What is the hottest planet in our solar system?

▲▲▲▲▲▲▲▲▲▲▲▲▲▲▲

713. When William Herschel discovered Uranus in 1781, what did he think it was?

a. a comet   b. a moon

c. a planet   d. a star

Answers: 699. hydrogen; 700. b; 701. a; 702. b; 703. true; 704. elliptical; 705. red giant; 706. Mercury; 707. Neptune; 708. false, Russian cosmonaut Valeri Polyakov once spent 437 straight days aboard the Mir space station; 709. more, 181; 710. b; 711. d; 712. Venus; 713. a

Scientific Knowledge • 69

714. Jupiter and _ _ _ _ _ _ are the two biggest planets in our solar system.

  a. Mars   b. Neptune
  c. Saturn   d. Uranus

715. The Olympus Mons is a large volcanic mountain on which planet?
  a. Mars
  b. Neptune
  c. Saturn
  d. Uranus

716. Is a year on Mercury shorter or longer than one on Earth?

718. HOW MANY MEN HAVE WALKED ON THE SURFACE OF THE MOON?
  A. 6   B. 8
  C. 10   D. 12

TOUGH TRIVIA CHALLENGE

717. What golf club did Alan Shepard use when he hit a ball on the Moon in 1971?
  a. driver
  b. 3-iron
  c. 6-iron
  d. pitching wedge

719. True or false? The average temperature on the moon is above 100°C during the day and less than -100°C at night.

MATCH THE ELEMENT TO ITS SYMBOL.

720. Silicon	a. Sn	
721. Nitrogen	b. Na	
722. Neon	c. B	
723. Gold	d. N	
724. Lithium	e. Fe	
725. Potassium	f. Ne	
726. Lead	g. K	
727. Mercury	h. Au	
728. Iodine	i. Cu	
729. Copper	j. H	
730. Helium	k. I	
731. Sodium	l. He	
732. Tin	m. Li	
733. Iron	n. Hg	
734. Boron	o. Si	
735. Hydrogen	p. Pb	

Answers: 714. c; 715. a; 716. shorter, just under 88 days total; 717. c; 718. d; 719. true; 720. o; 721. d; 722. f; 723. h; 724. m; 725. g; 726. p; 727. n; 728. k; 729. i; 730. l; 731. b; 732. a; 733. e; 734. c; 735. j

Scientific Knowledge • 71

736. Does the Earth contain more aluminum or silicon?

737. Does the Earth contain more iron or silicon?

738. Does the Earth contain more aluminum or iron?

739. Does the Earth contain more sodium or calcium?

740. DOES THE EARTH CONTAIN MORE MAGNESIUM OR POTASSIUM?

741. Silicon is used extensively in what technology?

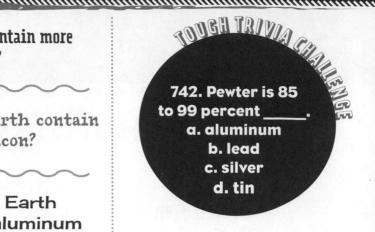

742. Pewter is 85 to 99 percent _____.
a. aluminum
b. lead
c. silver
d. tin

743. What are the three states of matter in all normal environments?

744. What is the process of a solid changing into a liquid called?

745. What is the process of a gas changing into a liquid called?

746. What is the process of a solid changing into a gas called?

747. WATER BOILS AT WHAT TEMPERATURE CELSIUS?

748. Water freezes at what temperature Celsius?

749. Morning dew is an example of which of the following?
a. transpiration
b. evaporation
c. precipitation
d. condensation

750. What is the center of an atom called?

752. Electric power is typically measured in what unit?

753. What is the wire inside an electric lightbulb known as?
a. cable
b. circuit
c. filament
d. transformer

751. A nuclear reaction where the nucleus of an atom splits into smaller parts is known as nuclear _____.
a. bifurcation   b. collapse   c. divorce   d. fission

Answers: 736. silicon; 737. silicon; 738. aluminum; 739. sodium; 740. magnesium; 741. computers; 742. d; 743. Solid, liquid, and gas; 744. melting; 745. condensation; 746. sublimation; 747. 100°C; 748. 0°C; 749. d; 750. nucleus; 751. d; 752. watts; 753. c.

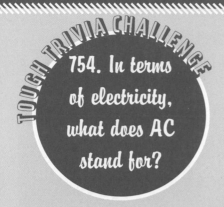

754. In terms of electricity, what does AC stand for?

755. True or false? You can extend the life of a battery by storing it at low temperatures.

. . . .

756. Infrared light cannot be seen by humans because its wavelength is too long or too short?

. . . .

757. What is a substance that does not conduct heat known as?
a. isolator
b. inoculator
c. insulator
d. insinuator

758. When heat is transferred through a solid object it is known as _____.
a. conduction
b. convection
c. radiation
d. transparation

759. IF YOU MELT 50 GRAMS OF ICE IN 150 GRAMS OF WATER, HOW MUCH WATER WILL YOU END UP WITH?

INVENTIONS & DISCOVERIES

760. The process of pasteurization is named after which famous French microbiologist?

761. Thanks to Alfred Nobel (yes, the one that the prize is named for), the world became way more explosive. What did he invent?

762. _____ and _____ Wright gave man the ability to fly.

763. Alessandro Volta developed the first _____ in the 19th century.
        a. battery
        b. light bulb
        c. microwave oven
        d. toaster

Answers: 754. alternating current; 755. true; 756. too long; 757. c; 758. a; 759. 200 grams; 760. Louis Pasteur; 761. dynamite; 762. Orville & Wilbur; 763. a.

Scientific Knowledge • 75

764. WHO INVENTED THE TELEPHONE?

766. What group of islands were studied extensively by Charles Darwin and led to his formulation of the theory of evolution?

    a. Faroe Islands

    b. Galapagos Islands

    c. Hawaiian Islands

    d. Canary Islands

TOUGH TRIVIA CHALLENGE

765. What woman is the only individual who was awarded a Nobel Prize in two different scientific fields?

767. Which discovery helped determine the age of the Earth?

    a. gravity

    b. radioactivity

    c. nuclear power

    d. atomic power

MATCH THE SCIENTIST(S) WITH THEIR REVOLUTIONARY DISCOVERY OR INVENTION.

768. Robert Wilson & Arno Penzias

769. Jonas Salk

770. Isaac Newton

771. Johannes Kepler

772. Ladislao Biro

773. James Watson & Francis Crick

774. Dmitry Mendeleev

775. J.J. Thomson

776. William Herschel

777. Albert Einstein

778. William Harvey

779. Gregor Mendel

780. Benjamin Franklin

781. Alexander Fleming

782. Nicholas Copernicus

783. Johannes Gutenberg

784. Edwin Hubble

785. Thomas Edison

786. James Prescott Joule

787. Antoine Lavoisier

788. Michael Faraday

a. discovery of other galaxies beyond the Milky Way

b. the electron

c. the role of oxygen in combustion

d. the double-helix structure of DNA

e. the Earth revolves around the sun

f. ballpoint pen

g. gravity

h. electricity

i. relativity

j. The Big Bang Theory

k. bifocals

l. penicillin

m. Periodic Table

n. polio vaccine

o. circulation of blood

p. infrared

q. genetic inheritance

r. First Law of Thermodynamics (Conservation of Energy)

s. Laws of Planetary Motion

t. printing press

u. light bulb

Answers: 764 Alexander Graham Bell; 765 Marie Curie; 766. b; 767 b; 768. j; 769. n; 770. g; 771. s; 772. f; 773. d; 774. m; 775. b; 776. p; 777. i; 778. o; 779. q; 780. k; 781. l; 782. e; 783. t; 784. a; 785. u; 786. r; 787. c; 788. h

Scientific Knowledge • 77

COMPUTERS

789. In terms of computing, what does CPU stand for?

790. In terms of computing, what does RAM stand for?

791. True or false? IBM stands for Intelligent Business Machines.

792. True or false? The ENIAC, one of the first electronic computers, weighed more than 25 tons.

794. _____ is the general term for harmful software like viruses, worms, and spyware.

TOUGH TRIVIA CHALLENGE

793. Which British inventor is known as the "Father of the Computer," for designing a mechanical computer called the Analytical Engine?
a. Alan Turing
b. Basil Rathbone
c. Charles Babbage
d. Michael Faraday

795. What science fiction writer invented the three laws of robotics?

a. Arthur C. Clarke
b. Isaac Asimov
c. Philip K. Dick
d. Ray Bradbury

796. HOW MANY EMPLOYEES DID TWITTER HAVE IN 2008?

A. 3
B. 8
C. 20
D. 32

MATCH THE SYMBOL TO THE KEY ON A STANDARD COMPUTER KEYBOARD.

797. (	a. 1
798. #	b. 2
799. !	c. 3
800. &	d. 4
801. $	e. 5
802. *	f. 6
803. ^	g. 7
804. @	h. 8
805.)	i. 9
806. %	j. 0

807. Thanks to Robert Cailliau and Tim Berners-Lee, you can go surfing in your home. What did they invent?

Answers: 789. Central Processing Unit; 790. Random-Access Memory; 791. false; 792. true; 793. c; 794. Malware; 795. b; 796. b; 797. i; 798. c; 799. c; 800. g; 801. d; 802. h; 803. f; 804. b; 805. j; 806. e; 807. the world wide web

OH, THE HUMANITY!

808. Every neuron in the human brain contains how many synapses?
- a. between 10 and 100
- b. between 100 and 1,000
- c. between 1,000 and 10,000
- d. between 10,000 and 100,000

809. What percentage of the oxygen in your body does your brain use?
- a. 10%
- b. 20%
- c. 30%
- d. 40%

810. What is another name for your "funny bone"?
- a. tibia
- b. patella
- c. humerus
- d. phalange

811. True or false? It is possible to tickle yourself.

812. Does your brain have more white matter (dendrites and axons) or gray matter (neurons)?

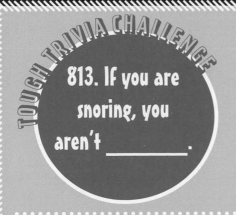

813. If you are snoring, you aren't _____.

814. Approximately how many nerve cells are there in the brain?

 a. 100 thousand
 b. 100 million
 c. 100 billion
 d. 100 trillion

MATCH THE BRAIN LOBE TO WHAT INFORMATION IS PROCESSED THERE.

815. frontal
816. parietal
817. occipital
818. temporal

a. vision
b. speech and thought
c. temperature and pain
d. hearing and memory

819. What is the name of the largest part of the human brain?

 a. cerebellum
 b. cerebrum
 c. hypothalamus
 d. pituitary

820. What is the name of the substance that gives human skin and hair its pigment?

 a. collagen
 b. keratin
 c. melanin
 d. sebum

Answers: 808. c; 809. b; 810. c; 811. false, the brain can separate touch by yourself and by someone else; 812. white matter; 813. dreaming; 814. c; 815. b; 816. c; 817. a; 818. d; 819. b; 820. c.

Scientific Knowledge • 87

821. What substance are a human's nails made out of?

a. collagen   b. keratin

c. melanin   d. sebum

▲▲▲▲▲▲▲▲▲▲▲▲

823. Another name for nose hair is _____.

a. cicilia   b. cilia   c. cellulite   d. cicily

▲▲▲▲▲▲▲▲▲▲▲▲▲▲▲▲▲▲

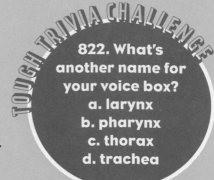

TOUGH TRIVIA CHALLENGE

822. What's another name for your voice box?

a. larynx
b. pharynx
c. thorax
d. trachea

MATCH THE TERM WITH ITS ASSOCIATED FEAR.

824. ablutophobia	a. fear of blood
825. acrophobia	b. fear of teenagers
826. androphobia	c. fear of clocks
827. arachnophobia	d. fear of bathing
828. arithmophobia	e. fear of birds
829. autophobia	f. fear of Halloween
830. bibliophobia	g. fear of books
831. chronomentrophobia	h. fear of fire
832. coulrophobia	i. fear of clowns
833. dendrophobia	j. fear of numbers
834. domatophobia	k. fear of trees
835. ephebiphobia	l. fear of animals
836. equinophobia	m. fear of houses
837. genuphobia	n. fear of the dark
838. hemophobia	o. fear of the figure 8
839. hypochondria	p. fear of strangers or foreigners
840. nyctophobia	q. fear of men
841. octophobia	r. fear of illness
842. orinthophobia	s. fear of heights
843. pyrophobia	t. fear of horses
844. samhainophobia	u. fear of knees
845. tachophobia	v. fear of being alone
846. xenophobia	w. fear of spiders
847. zoophobia	x. fear of speed

848. What is the common term for the medical condition known as hypertension?
   a. anxiety
   b. muscle tightness
   c. depression
   d. high blood pressure

849. The disease tuberculosis was formerly known as _____.
   a. scurvy
   b. consumption
   c. leprosy
   d. smallpox

850. True or false?

Your pinkie toe is crucial to your balance.

851. HUMAN DNA IS WHAT SHAPE?

852. A single piece of coiled DNA is known as a _____.
   a. belt
   b. chromosome
   c. helix
   d. nucleotide

TOUGH TRIVIA CHALLENGE

853. The outer layer of a human cell is the _____?
   a. vacuole
   b. cytoplasm
   c. cell wall
   d. cell membrane

CHAPTER 3

Cultural Cachet

854. What computer industry titan helped found Pixar?

   a. Larry Ellison   b. Bill Gates

   c. Steve Jobs   d. Steve Wozniak

855. True or false? The voice of the little girl in *Monsters, Inc.* was supplied by the 2-year-old daughter of one of the animators.

856. Which of the following Pixar classics did not win the Academy Award for Best Animated Feature?

   a. *Ratatouille*   b. *Monsters, Inc.*

   c. *Finding Nemo*   d. *Toy Story 3*

857. What is Mr. Incredible's job when he is not working as a superhero?

a. advertising executive

b. cook

c. insurance adjuster

d. truck driver

DO YOU SELL LIFE INSURANCE POLICIES FOR MINIONS?

859. What is the name of the robot Wall-E falls in love with?
a. Eleanor
b. Elizabeth
c. Emma
d. Eve

860. What is the name of the girl in *Inside Out*?
a. Boo
b. Colette
c. Riley
d. Zooey

TOUGH TRIVIA CHALLENGE

862. *Cars* has been criticized of ripping off the plot to which Michael J. Fox movie?
a. *Back to the Future*
b. *Teen Wolf*
c. *Doc Hollywood*
d. *Bright Lights, Big City*

861. What is the name of the kindly great white shark in *Finding Nemo*?
a. Bruce
b. Hank
c. Keith
d. Roger

863. Who was the first actor to perform live (aka not animated) in a Pixar movie?

    a. Yahoo Serious
    b. Fred Willard
    c. Janeane Garofalo
    d. Patton Oswalt

864. What is the primary ingredient in ratatouille?

    a. cabbage
    b. cheese
    c. eggplant
    d. rat

865. As of 2018, what actor has supplied at least one voice in every Pixar movie?

a. Joan Cusack
b. John Goodman
c. John Ratzenberger
d. Brad Garrett

866. WHAT NOTORIOUS DESTROYER OF TOYS LIVES NEXT DOOR TO ANDY IN TOY STORY?

A. EDNA
B. ARLO
C. VIOLET
D. SID

867. JOSS WHEDON, WHO WROTE AND DIRECTED THE FIRST TWO AVENGERS MOVIES, ALSO HELPED WRITE WHICH PIXAR CLASSIC?

868. True or False? Disney almost ended production on *Toy Story* because they felt Woody was too sarcastic.

◆◆◆

869. *Up, Toy Story 3,* and Disney's _____ are the only animated films to ever be nominated for Best Picture at the Academy Awards.
   a. *Bambi*
   b. *Beauty and the Beast*
   c. *The Lion King*
   d. *Pinocchio*

◆◆◆

870. PUT THESE FIVE EARLY DISNEY MOVIES IN ORDER OF THEIR FIRST THEATRICAL RELEASE.
   A. *PINOCCHIO*
   B. *DUMBO*
   C. *BAMBI*
   D. *SNOW WHITE AND THE SEVEN DWARFS*
   E. *FANTASIA*

◆◆◆

871. Who wrote the original story of *The Little Mermaid?*
   a. The Brothers Grimm
   b. Hans Christian Andersen
   c. Edgar Allan Poe
   d. H.G. Wells

872. In *The Little Mermaid*, the potion turns Ariel into a human for how many days?

    a. 1   b. 2

    c. 3   d. 4

874. In what country does Disney's *Beauty and the Beast* take place?

TOUGH TRIVIA CHALLENGE

873. In *Beauty and the Beast*, what is Gaston "especially good at"?

875. Belle from *Beauty and the Beast* makes a brief appearance in what other Disney film?

876. IN *PETER PAN*, IS CAPTAIN HOOK'S HOOK ATTACHED TO HIS LEFT OR RIGHT ARM?

877. In *Hercules*, the title character's credit card has an expiration date of M BC. What year is that?

MATCH THE VILLAIN TO THE MOVIE.

878. Cruella de Vil
879. Dr. Facilier
880. Frollo
881. Gaston
882. Hades
883. Jafar
884. Madame Medusa
885. Maleficent
886. Man
887. Governor Ratcliffe
888. Professor Ratigan
889. Scar
890. Shan Yu
891. Shere Khan
892. Stromboli
893. Sykes
894. Ursula

a. *101 Dalmatians*
b. *Aladdin*
c. *Bambi*
d. *Beauty and the Beast*
e. *The Great Mouse Detective*
f. *Hercules*
g. *The Hunchback of Notre Dame*
h. *The Jungle Book*
i. *The Lion King*
j. *The Little Mermaid*
k. *Mulan*
l. *Oliver and Company*
m. *Pinocchio*
n. *Pocahontas*
o. *The Princess and the Frog*
p. *The Rescuers*
q. *Sleeping Beauty*

895. What historical event knocked Dumbo off of the cover of *Time* magazine in December 1941?

I AM YOUR FATHER!

896. James Earl Jones provided the voice of Mufasa in *The Lion King*. He also provided the voice for which famous villain?

··FILM··

Three films are tied for the record for most Academy Awards, with 11. Name the film that _ _ _ _ _ _.

897. had a big scene involving a chariot race
898. climaxed with the sinking of an ocean liner
899. was the third film in a series

900. What silent movie star was known as "The Little Tramp"?

901. True or false? Jimmy Stewart never won an Academy Award for Best Actor.

902. Jack Nicholson and _____ are the only two men to win three Academy Awards for Best Actor.
a. Marlon Brando
b. Daniel Day-Lewis
c. Spencer Tracy
d. Denzel Washington

903. Who has won more Academy Awards for Best Actress, Katharine Hepburn or Meryl Streep?

904. Who has more Academy Award nominations, Katharine Hepburn or Meryl Streep?

905. Julie Andrews won the Academy Award for Best Actress for the first movie she was in. What was the movie?

906. John Williams has the most Academy Award nominations of any living person. What is his job?

a. composing
b. directing
c. acting
d. costume design

TOUGH TRIVIA CHALLENGE

907. Marion Cotillard won an Academy Award for portraying which singer in 2007?
a. Debbie Harry
b. Edith Piaf
c. Diana Ross
d. Britney Spears

MATCH THE DIRECTOR WITH THEIR FAMOUS WORK.

908. Kathryn Bigelow

909. Francis Ford Coppola

910. Frank Capra

911. Steven Spielberg

912. Ridley Scott

913. Wes Anderson

914. James Cameron

915. Orson Welles

916. Alfred Hitchcock

917. Stanley Kubrick

918. Christopher Nolan

919. Charlie Chaplin

a. *Fantastic Mr. Fox*

b. *Point Break*

c. *Titanic*

d. *It's a Wonderful Life*

e. *Blade Runner*

f. *City Lights*

g. *Citizen Kane*

h. *Batman Begins*

i. *The Godfather*

j. *Jaws*

k. *Rear Window*

l. *2001: A Space Odyssey*

920. What is the name of the modern version of *A Christmas Carol* starring Bill Murray?

a. *Marley & Me*
b. *Scrooged*
c. *Merry Christmas, Mr. Scrooge*
d. *Uncle Ebenezer*

921. Which star of the 2001 hit *Ocean's Eleven* was also the voice of Mr. Fox in *Fantastic Mr. Fox*?

a. Don Cheadle
b. George Clooney
c. Matt Damon
d. Brad Pitt

TOUGH TRIVIA CHALLENGE

922. Norma Jean Baker is better known as whom?

a. Sally Field
b. Katharine Hepburn
c. Marilyn Monroe
d. Joanne Woodward

923. Joanne Woodward, who won an Academy Award for Best Actress in 1957, was married to which screen legend for 50 years?

a. Warren Beatty
b. Marlon Brando
c. Paul Newman
d. Al Pacino

924. TRUE OR FALSE? Actor Sylvester Stallone, who stars in *Rocky*, also wrote the screenplay.

925. Name the two rival gangs in *West Side Story*.

a. Oil and Water
b. Ghosts and Spirits
c. Sharks and Jets
d. none of the above

COMPLETE THE TITLES OF THESE FILMS, WHICH HAVE BEEN DEEMED "CULTURALLY, HISTORICALLY OR AESTHETICALLY SIGNIFICANT" BY THE LIBRARY OF CONGRESS' NATIONAL FILM REGISTRY.

926. _____ *of the Sierra Madre*

927. *The Great Train _____*

928. *All Quiet on the Western _____*

929. *Lawrence of _____*

930. *2001: A Space _____*

931. *Bonnie and _____*

932. *Sweet Smell of _____*

933. *One Flew Over the _____ Nest*

934. *Blade _____*

935. *To Kill a _____*

936. *North by _____*

937. *The Day the Earth Stood _____*

938. _____ *Graffiti*

939. *The Outlaw Josie _____*

940. *West Side _____*

941. *How the West Was _____*

942. *The Bridge on the _____ Kwai*

943. *A Streetcar Named _____*

944. *Raiders of the Lost _____*

945. *Night of the Living _____*

946. *Do the Right _____*

947. *Apocalypse _____*

948. *The Sound of _____*

949. *In the Heat of the _____*

950. *Butch Cassidy and the _____ Kid*

951. *A Raisin in the _____*

952. *Miracle on _____ Street*

953. *The French _____*

954. *Cool Hand _____*

955. *Close Encounters of the Third _____*

956. *12 Angry _____*

957. *In Cold _____*

958. *Dog Day _____*

959. *A Tree Grows in _____*

960. *The Empire Strikes _____*

961. *All the _____ Men*

962. *Sunset _____*

963. *Some Like It _____*

964. *Mr. Smith Goes to _____*

965. *The Grapes of _____*

966. *Citizen _____*

967. *Rebel Without a _____*

968. *Raging _____*

969. *All _____ Eve*

970. *Duck _____*

971. What is Voldemort's given name?

972. What monster did Salazar Slytherin place inside the Chamber of Secrets?
- a. basilisk
- b. cerberus
- c. dragon
- d. werewolf

TOUGH TRIVIA CHALLENGE

974. When is Harry Potter's birthday?
- a. August 8th
- b. February 29th
- c. June 1st
- d. July 31st

973. What is the name of the language that snakes speak?

975. WHAT DOES HARRY TAKE TO COMPETE IN THE SECOND CHALLENGE OF THE TRIWIZARD TOURNAMENT?

976. What position does Harry play in Quidditch?

- - - - - - -

977. Who is Harry's godfather?
a. Albus Dumbledore
b. Remus Lupin
c. Severus Snape
d. Sirius Black

- - - - - - -

978. Harry's wand is made out of holly and a _____?

- - - - - - -

979. What does Harry see in the Mirror of Erised?
a. Ginny Weasley
b. himself defeating Voldemort
c. his parents
d. the golden snitch

980. What is the name of Dumbledore's pet phoenix?
a. Hedwig
b. Fawkes
c. Percy
d. Sonny

981. What are Hermione Granger's parents employed as?
a. dentists
b. doctors
c. lawyers
d. professors

- - - - - - -

982. How many brothers does Ron Weasley have?
a. 3
b. 4
c. 5
d. 6

Answers: 971. Tom Riddle; 972. a; 973. parseltongue; 974. d; 975. gillyweed; 976. seeker; 977. d; 978. phoenix feather; 979. c; 980. b; 981. a; 982. c

Cultural Cachet • **97**

983. WHICH ONE OF RON'S BROTHERS DIES, FRED OR GEORGE?

984. What is Ron's father's name?
    a. Ace   b. Adam
    c. Albus   d. Arthur

985. What department in the Ministry of Magic did Arthur Weasley work in when Cornelius Fudge was the Minister of Magic?

986. What is J.K. Rowling's first name?
    a. Jane   b. Joanne
    c. Kimberly   d. Marena

987. What is Professor McGonagall's first name?
    a. Marica   b. Minerva
    c. Thetis   d. Medusa

988. True or false? Dame Maggie Smith, who plays Professor McGonagall in the Harry Potter movies, has an Academy Award for Best Actress.

989. The Patronus Charm should be used if one encounters _ _ _ _ _ _ _.

990. WHO IS NAGINI?

991. What does Voldemort steal from Dumbledore's grave?

992. What subject does Severus Snape always want to teach?

a. Potions
b. Defense Against the Dark Arts
c. Transfiguration
d. Divination

993. Who is the "Half-Blood Prince"?

WORKING IN THE ORDER THEY WERE RELEASED, COMPLETE THE TITLES OF THE HARRY POTTER NOVELS.

994. *Harry Potter and _____ (1997)*
995. *Harry Potter and _____ (1998)*
996. *Harry Potter and _____ (1999)*
997. *Harry Potter and _____ (2000)*
998. *Harry Potter and _____ (2003)*
999. *Harry Potter and _____ (2005)*
1000. *Harry Potter and _____ (2007)*

Answers: 983. Fred; 984. d; 985. Misuse of Muggle Artifacts; 986. b; 987. b; 988. true, for 1969's *The Prime of Miss Jean Brodie*; 989. Dementors; 990. Voldemort's snake; 991. the elder wand; 992. b; 993. Severus Snape; 994. *the Philosopher's (or Sorcerer's) Stone*; 995. *the Chamber of Secrets*; 996. *the Prisoner of Azkaban*; 997. *the Goblet of Fire*; 998. *the Order of the Phoenix*; 999. *the Half-Blood Prince*; 1000. *the Deathly Hallows*

1001. The author of *The Wonderful Wizard of Oz* is L. Frank Baum. What does the L stand for?

        a. Leon
        b. Leonard
        c. Lion
        d. Lyman

1002. What state is Dorothy from in *The Wizard of Oz*?

1003. What Broadway musical tells a witch's side of the Wizard of Oz story?

TOUGH TRIVIA CHALLENGE

1004. What other classic movie beat out *The Wizard of Oz* for Best Picture at the 1939 Academy Awards?

1005. Who wrote the first major time travel novel, H.G. Wells or Mark Twain?

MATCH THE AUTHOR
WITH THEIR FAMOUS WORK.

1006. JOHN STEINBECK

1007. WILLIAM
SHAKESPEARE

1008. LEWIS CARROLL

1009. C.S. LEWIS

1010. LEO TOLSTOY

1011. E.B. WHITE

1012. LOIS LOWRY

1013. J.D. SALINGER

1014. JONATHAN SWIFT

1015. JANE AUSTEN

1016. GEORGE ORWELL

1017. MARK TWAIN

1018. F. SCOTT
FITZGERALD

1019. HARPER
LEE

A. *THE LION, THE WITCH
AND THE WARDROBE*

B. *CHARLOTTE'S WEB*

C. *THE GIVER*

D. *TO KILL A MOCKINGBIRD*

E. *OF MICE AND MEN*

F. *GULLIVER'S TRAVELS*

G. *NINETEEN EIGHTY FOUR*

H. *PRIDE AND PREJUDICE*

I. *THE ADVENTURES OF
HUCKLEBERRY FINN*

J. *ALICE'S ADVENTURES IN
WONDERLAND*

K. *THE CATCHER IN THE RYE*

L. *THE GREAT GATSBY*

M. *HAMLET*

N. *WAR AND PEACE*

1020. Which of J.R.R. Tolkien's famously tiny literary characters celebrate their birthdays on September 22nd?

1021. What is the relationship between Bilbo and Frodo Baggins?

1022. What book is Veruca Salt a character in?

1023. What Charles Dickens character is famous for saying: "Please, sir, I want some more"?

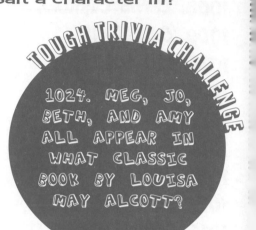

TOUGH TRIVIA CHALLENGE

1024. MEG, JO, BETH, AND AMY ALL APPEAR IN WHAT CLASSIC BOOK BY LOUISA MAY ALCOTT?

1025. True or false? The heavy metal band in the *Diary of a Wimpy Kid* books is called Löded Diper.

1026. Gabriel, Michael, and _____ are the only angels mentioned by name in the Bible.

1027. In Winnie the Pooh, how is acre spelled on the map of the 100 Acre Woods?

1028. In *Alice in Wonderland* who says, "Everybody has won, and all must have prizes"?
  a. The March Hare
  b. The Mad Hatter
  c. The Dodo
  d. The Mock Turtle

1029. WHICH LEGENDARY IRISH WRITER HAD "NOTHING TO DECLARE EXCEPT MY GENIUS" AT U.S. CUSTOMS?
  A. JAMES JOYCE
  B. SAMUEL BECKETT
  C. OSCAR WILDE
  D. W.B. YEATS

1030. Bram Stoker's *Dracula* is an epistolary novel. What does that mean?
  a. It's scary
  b. It's written as a series of letters and other documents
  c. There are many narrators
  d. It has been translated into more than five languages

1031. In the novel *Dracula*, Dracula's castle is located in what mountain range?
  a. Allegheny Mountains
  b. Sierra Madre Mountains
  c. The Alps
  d. Carpathian Mountains

1032. Who is the author of *The Jungle Book*?

1033. What country was Sherlock Holmes author Sir Arthur Conan Doyle from?
  a. England
  b. Ireland
  c. Scotland
  d. Wales

Answers: 1020. Bilbo and Frodo Baggins; 1021. Bilbo is Frodo's uncle; 1022. *Charlie and the Chocolate Factory*; 1023. Oliver Twist; 1024. *Little Women*; 1025. true; 1026. Lucifer, a "fallen angel" who God cast out of heaven; 1027. Aker; 1028. c; 1029. c; 1030. b; 1031. d; 1032. Rudyard Kipling; 1033. c.

Cultural Cachet • **103**

1034. The first Sherlock Holmes adventure was called what?
a. *A Picture in Pink*
b. *A Study in Scarlet*
c. *A Clue in Blue*
d. *A Scene in Green*

1035. Who narrates most of the Sherlock Holmes stories?

1036. On what street in London does Sherlock Holmes live?

1037. What is Sherlock Holmes's older brother's name?

1038. In the story "His Last Bow," Sherlock Holmes has retired and become a _____.
a. baker
b. beekeeper
c. bus driver
d. butcher

1039. WHO WROTE THE PHANTOM TOLLBOOTH?

1040. Who wrote *Mr. Popper's Penguins?*

1041. Who wrote *Harriet the Spy?*

1042. Who wrote *Matilda?*

1043. Who wrote *Bridge to Terabithia?*

1044. In the Winnie the Pooh stories, what is Kanga's baby called?

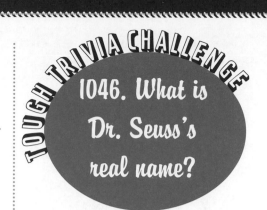

TOUGH TRIVIA CHALLENGE

1046. What is Dr. Seuss's real name?

1047. Horton the Elephant lives in the Jungle of _____.
a. **Fool**
b. **Kool**
c. **Nool**
d. **Thtool**

1048. On what mountain does The Grinch live?

1045. WHICH OF THE FOLLOWING WAS NOT WRITTEN BY JULES VERNE?
a. *Twenty Thousand Leagues Under the Sea*   b. *Journey to the Center of the Earth*
c. *The War of the Worlds*   d. *Around the World in 80 Days*

1049. How many sizes does the Grinch's heart grow at the end of the book?

1050. WHAT DOES THE LORAX SPEAK FOR?
   A. THE OCEANS
   B. THE STARS
   C. THE ANIMALS
   D. THE TREES

TOUGH TRIVIA CHALLENGE

1051. What legendary children's author also wrote the hit Johnny Cash song "A Boy Named Sue"?
   a. Dr. Seuss
   b. Roald Dahl
   c. Shel Silverstein
   d. Maurice Sendak

1052. TRUE OR FALSE? FAMOUS CHILDREN'S AUTHOR ROALD DAHL ALSO WROTE A SCREENPLAY FOR A JAMES BOND FILM.

1053. What radio DJ coined the term rock 'n' roll?
- a. Dick Clark
- b. Alan Freed
- c. Wolfman Jack
- d. Casey Kasem

1054. What is Paul McCartney's actual first name?

TOUGH TRIVIA CHALLENGE

1055. What was The Beatles' name before they became The Beatles?
- a. The Hamburg Four
- b. The Lenins
- c. The Quarrymen
- d. The Shaggs

1056. Which Beatle was on the cover of the first *Rolling Stone*?

1057. In April of 1964, the Beatles held the first _____ spots on the Billboard Hot 100.
- a. 2
- b. 3
- c. 4
- d. 5

1058. True or false? Led Zeppelin was once called the Warlocks.

1059. In what American city did grunge rock originate?

Answers: 1049, 3; 1050, d; 1051, c; 1052, true, 1967's *You Only Live Twice*; 1053, b; 1054, James; 1055, c; 1056, John Lennon; 1057, d; 1058, false, the Grateful Dead were once known as the Warlocks; 1059, Seattle

MATCH THE LEAD SINGER WITH THEIR BAND.

1060. MICK JAGGER

1061. ROBERT PLANT

1062. BONO

1063. BRUCE SPRINGSTEEN

1064. ANNIE LENNOX

1065. ROGER DALTREY

1066. JERRY GARCIA

1067. CHRISSIE HYNDE

1068. JIM MORRISON

1069. STEVEN TYLER

1070. BRIAN WILSON

1071. DAVID LEE ROTH

1072. DAVID BYRNE

1073. DENNIS EDWARDS

1074. KURT COBAIN

1075. FREDDIE MERCURY

1076. THOM YORKE

1077. MICHAEL JACKSON

1078. DIANA ROSS

1079. BEYONCE KNOWLES

A. TALKING HEADS

B. RADIOHEAD

C. EURYTHMICS

D. THE PRETENDERS

E. THE ROLLING STONES

F. DESTINY'S CHILD

G. THE BEACH BOYS

H. LED ZEPPELIN

I. U2

J. THE E STREET BAND

K. THE WHO

L. VAN HALEN

M. NIRVANA

N. THE DOORS

O. QUEEN

P. GRATEFUL DEAD

Q. AEROSMITH

R. THE TEMPTATIONS

S. JACKSON 5

T. THE SUPREMES

1080. Which of the following is not a legendary bass player?

    a. John Entwistle
    b. Tina Weymouth
    c. Randy Rhoads
    d. Phil Lesh

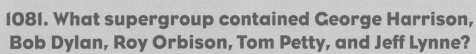

1081. What supergroup contained George Harrison, Bob Dylan, Roy Orbison, Tom Petty, and Jeff Lynne?

    a. Van Halen
    b. Oysterhead
    c. Chickenfoot
    d. Traveling Wilburys

1082. What future pop superstar was born in Barbados in 1988?

1083. What is the name of Eminem's alter ego?

1084. Charlie Watts is the drummer for what legendary band?

Answers: 1060. e; 1061. h; 1062. i; 1063. j; 1064. c; 1065. k; 1066. p; 1067. d; 1068. n; 1069. q; 1070. g; 1071. l; 1072. a; 1073. r; 1074. m; 1075. o; 1076. b; 1077. s; 1078. t; 1079. f; 1080. c; 1081. d; 1082. Rihanna; 1083. Slim Shady; 1084. The Rolling Stones

Cultural Cachet • 109

1085. Which U2 album came first, *The Joshua Tree* or *Achtung Baby*?

▲▲▲▲▲▲▲▲▲▲▲▲▲▲▲

TOUGH TRIVIA CHALLENGE

1086. What soul legend wrote "Respect," which Aretha Franklin took to #1 in the U.S. in 1967?
a. Ray Charles
b. Al Green
c. Otis Redding
d. Bill Withers

▲▲▲▲▲▲▲▲▲▲▲▲▲▲▲

1087. Robert Zimmerman is the real name of which iconic musician?
a. Bob Dylan
b. Buddy Holly
c. Elvis Presley
d. Stevie Wonder

▲▲▲▲▲▲▲▲▲▲▲▲▲

1088. What folk singer wrote "This Land Is Your Land"?
a. Bob Dylan
b. Woody Guthrie
c. Lead Belly
d. Dave Van Ronk

▲▲▲▲▲▲▲▲▲▲▲▲▲▲

1089. What band is the subject of the 1984 documentary *Stop Making Sense?*
a. Van Halen
b. Talking Heads
c. The Police
d. The Thompson Twins

▲▲▲▲▲▲▲▲▲▲▲▲▲▲

1090. Who is the only artist to have a Top 10 hit with "The Star Spangled Banner"?
a. Whitney Houston
b. Marvin Gaye
c. Ariana Grande
d. Kelly Clarkson

▲▲▲▲▲▲▲▲▲▲▲▲

MATCH THE FILM TO THE MUSICIAN WHO IS THE SUBJECT OF IT.

1091. *Coal Miner's Daughter*

1092. *La Bamba*

1093. *Walk the Line*

1094. *Great Balls of Fire*

1095. *What's Love Got to Do With It*

1096. *Why Do Fools Fall in Love*

1097. *Bohemian Rhapsody*

1098. *Sweet Dreams*

1099. *Nowhere Boy*

a. Jerry Lee Lewis

b. Frankie Lymon

c. Freddie Mercury

d. Richie Valens

e. John Lennon

f. Loretta Lynn

g. Tina Turner

h. Johnny Cash

i. Patsy Cline

Answers: 1085. *The Joshua Tree*: 1086. c; 1087. a; 1088. b; 1089. b; 1090. a; 1091. f; 1092. d; 1093. h; 1094. a; 1095. g; 1096. b; 1097. c; 1098. i; 1099. e

Cultural Cachet • 111

MATCH THE CLASSIC SONG TO THE ARTIST.

1100. "American Pie"

1101. "I Wanna Dance With Somebody"

1102. "Seven Nation Army"

1103. "Tangerine"

1104. "Karma Police"

1105. "Rockin' in the Free World"

1106. "Mr. Blue Sky"

1107. "Hey Jude"

1108. "Visions of Johanna"

1109. "Devil's Haircut"

1110. "Apocalypse Dreams"

1111. "Peaches en Regalia"

1112. "As"

1113. "Folsom Prison Blues"

1114. "Inner City Blues"

1115. "Umbrella"

1116. "At Last"

1117. "Everlong"

1118. "Blue Monday"

1119. "Rich Girl"

1120. "Changes"

1121. "Pretty Woman"

1122. "Heart of Glass"

1123. "That's the Way Love Goes"

1124. "Sorry"

a. Johnny Cash

b. Bob Dylan

c. Electric Light Orchestra

d. Blondie

e. Neil Young

f. Tame Impala

g. The Beatles

h. Justin Bieber

i. Roy Orbison

j. Rihanna

k. Marvin Gaye

l. Janet Jackson

m. Radiohead

n. David Bowie

o. Frank Zappa

p. Etta James

q. Foo Fighters

r. The White Stripes

s. Whitney Houston

t. Stevie Wonder

u. New Order

v. Don McLean

w. Led Zeppelin

x. Hall & Oates

y. Beck

1125. What Christmas song is the best-selling single (Christmas or otherwise) of all-time?
a. Mariah Carey's "All I Want for Christmas Is You"
b. Band Aid's "Do They Know It's Christmas?"
c. Elvis Presley's "Blue Christmas"
d. Bing Crosby's "White Christmas"

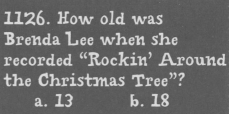

1126. How old was Brenda Lee when she recorded "Rockin' Around the Christmas Tree"?
a. 13   b. 18
c. 27   d. 41

1127. In what country did "Good King Wenceslas" rule?
a. Germany   b. Poland
c. Russia   d. Switzerland

Match the composer with their famous work.

1128. Bach	a. "Rhapsody in Blue"
1129. Handel	b. "Brandenburg Concertos"
1130. Beethoven	c. "The Minute Waltz"
1131. Chopin	d. "Appalachian Spring"
1132. Tchaikovsky	e. "Bolero"
1133. Dvorak	f. "From the New World"
1134. Holst	g. "The Planets"
1135. Ravel	h. "Messiah"
1136. Stravinsky	i. "The Firebird"
1137. Prokofiev	j. "The Nutcracker"
1138. Gershwin	k. "Pastoral Symphony"
1139. Copland	l. "Peter and the Wolf"

1140. *Fidelio* is the only opera by which legendary composer?
a. Bach
b. Beethoven
c. Mozart
d. Tchaikovsky

1141. How many parts make up Wagner's Ring Cycle?

a. 2

b. 4

c. 6

d. 8

1142. The lyrics of "Joy to the World" are taken from a _____.
a. greeting card
b. J.R.R. Tolkien novel
c. psalm
d. none of the above

1143. WHAT IS GIVEN ON THE SIXTH DAY IN "THE 12 DAYS OF CHRISTMAS"?

MYTHOLOGY

1144. How many gods lived on Mount Olympus?
- a. 12
- b. 54
- c. 140
- d. 300

- - - - - - - - -

1145. The mythological three-headed dog that guards the gates of Hades is named _____.
- a. Cerberus
- b. Centius
- c. Serpentus
- d. Scentilous

- - - - - - - - -

1146. True or false?
Cronus and Zeus are both Titans.

1147. If you cut off one of the heads of the _____, two more grow back.

TOUGH TRIVIA CHALLENGE

1148. The Minotaur and his labyrinth were located on which island?
a. Crete b. Delos
c. Rhodes d. Syracuse

1149. Who designed the labyrinth for King Minos, Odysseus, Perseus, or Daedalus?

Answers: 1140. b; 1141. b; 1142. c; 1143. geese-a-laying; 1144. a; 1145. a; 1146. false, Zeus is an Olympian; 1147. hydra; 1148. a; 1149. Daedalus

Cultural Cachet • 115

1150. Icarus's wings melted after he flew too close to what?

1151. Was Aphrodite or Iris the Greek goddess of the rainbow?

1152. In Greek mythology, is Charon the god of sleep or the ferryman of the underworld?

TOUGH TRIVIA CHALLENGE

1153. Which of the following is known as the "river of woe" in Greek mythology?
a. Achelous
b. Acheron
c. Actaeon
d. Aeolus

1154. What is the name of the Greek god of the sea?

1155. Centaurs are half man and half what?

1156. IS THE GOD PAN A CENTAUR OR SATYR?

1157. Harpies have the heads of human women and the bodies of what?

1158. Who was Hercules's father, Ares or Zeus?

1159. Who granted Cassandra the gift of prophecy, Apollo or Ares?

TOUGH TRIVIA CHALLENGE

1160. Who supervised the weighing of souls at judgment in Egyptian mythology, Anubis or Horus?

1161. In Egyptian mythology, what would go on the other side of the scale when one's soul was being weighed?

a. a cat
b. a feather
c. a gold coin
d. sand

Answers: 1150. the sun; 1151. Iris; 1152. ferryman of the underworld; 1153. b; 1154. Poseidon; 1155. horse; 1156. satyr; 1157. birds; 1158. Zeus; 1159. Apollo; 1160. Anubis; 1161. b

Match the artist to his or her country.

1162. René Magritte	**a. Austria**
1163. Gustav Klimt	**b. United States**
1164. Jasper Johns	**c. Belgium**
1165. Joan Miro	**d. Norway**
1166. Michelangelo	**e. Italy**
1167. Frida Kahlo	**f. Mexico**
1168. Claude Monet	**g. France**
1169. Edvard Munch	**h. Spain**

1170. True or false? **Michelangelo took more than 10 years to paint the ceiling of the Sistine Chapel.**

1171. Hue is another word for _____.

TOUGH TRIVIA CHALLENGE

1172. Kandinsky is generally regarded as the first _____ painter.
a. abstract
b. cubist
c. impressionist
d. pointillist

1173. True or false? Vincent Van Gogh only sold one painting during his life.

1174. Which artist was struck in the face with a mallet by an envious rival and disfigured for life?
a. Botticelli
b. Michelangelo
c. Raphael
d. Velazquez

Answers: 1162. c; 1163. a; 1164. b; 1165. h; 1166. e; 1167. f; 1168. g; 1169. d; 1170. false, it took four; 1171. color; 1172. a; 1173. true; 1174. b

Cultural Cachet • **119**

MATCH THE ARTWORK TO THE ARTIST.

1175. *The Moulin Rouge*

1176. *Girl with a Pearl Earring*

1177. *Campbell's Soup Cans*

1178. *Christina's World*

1179. *The Starry Night*

1180. *The Night Watch*

1181. *The Last Supper*

1182. *The Scream*

1183. *Guernica*

1184. *A Sunday Afternoon on the Island of La Grande Jatte*

a. Georges Seurat

b. Henri de Toulouse-Lautrec

c. Vincent Van Gogh

d. Edvard Munch

e. Andrew Wyeth

f. Johannes Vermeer

g. Pablo Picasso

h. Rembrandt

i. Leonardo Da Vinci

j. Andy Warhol

1185. True or false? Egg yolk was commonly utilized by classical painters.

1186. Which revered American architect designed the Guggenheim Museum, Frank Lloyd Wright or Frank Gehry?

COMICS

1187. WHAT DOES DC STAND FOR?
- A. DETECTIVE COMICS
- B. DELIGHTFUL COMICS
- C. DRIVE COMICS
- D. DRAWN COMICS

1188. Which came first: DC or Marvel?

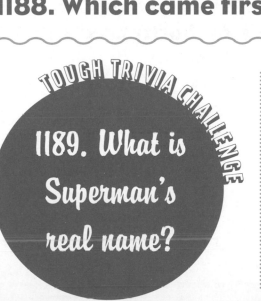

TOUGH TRIVIA CHALLENGE

1189. What is Superman's real name?

1190. Superman, Jimmy Olsen, Lois Lane, and Perry White all work for what newspaper?

1191. What super power does Mr. Fantastic have?

1192. What is the superhero name for Johnny Storm?

1193. When was the Comics Code Authority created?
- a. 1954
- b. 1960
- c. 1964
- d. 1970

1194. True or false? The Comics Code specifically restricted the ridicule of religion.

1195. What comic book was included on *Time* magazine's list of the 100 best English-language novels from 1923 to 2005?

MATCH THE COMIC BOOK CHARACTER TO THEIR SECRET IDENTITY.

1196. Bruce Banner

1197. Billy Batson

1198. Betsy Braddock

1199. Frank Castle

1200. Linda Danvers

1201. Barbara Gordon

1202. Dick Grayson

1203. Carter Hall

1204. James "Logan" Howlett

1205. Clark Kent

1206. Peter Parker

1207. Diana Prince

1208. Kyle Rayner

1209. Steve Rogers

1210. Albert Simmons

1211. Tony Stark

1212. Bruce Wayne

1213. Wally West

1214. Eel O'Brian

a. Batgirl

b. Batman

c. Captain America

d. Captain Marvel/ Shazam

e. The Flash

f. Green Lantern

g. Hawkman

h. The Incredible Hulk

i. Iron Man

j. Plastic-Man

k. Psylocke

l. The Punisher

m. Robin

n. Spawn

o. Spider-Man

p. Supergirl

q. Superman

r. Wolverine

s. Wonder Woman

1215. Peter Parker works as a photographer for the

_ _ _ _ _ _ .

a. *Boston Herald*
b. *Daily Planet*
c. *Daily Bugle*
d. *New York Times*

▲ ▲ ▲ ▲ ▲ ▲ ▲ ▲ ▲ ▲ ▲ ▲ ▲ ▲

1216. T'Challa, the king of Wakanda, is also known as _ _ _ _ _ .

▲ ▲ ▲ ▲ ▲ ▲ ▲ ▲ ▲ ▲ ▲ ▲ ▲ ▲

1217. Doctor Strange's home in Greenwich Village is known as

_ _ _ _ _ _ _

a. The Bowery
b. Darkmoor
c. Salem Center
d. Sanctum Santorum

1219. True or false? Wolverine is a founding member of the X-Men.

▲ ▲ ▲ ▲ ▲ ▲ ▲ ▲ ▲ ▲ ▲ ▲ ▲ ▲

1220. Michael Jackson tried to buy Marvel Comics in the 1990s because he wanted to play _ _ _ _ _ _ _ in a movie.

a. Captain America
b. Iron Man
c. The Incredible Hulk
d. Spider-Man

▲ ▲ ▲ ▲ ▲ ▲ ▲ ▲ ▲ ▲ ▲ ▲ ▲ ▲

1221. What member of the Avengers is Thanos's brother, Starfox, Captain Marvel, or Thor?

▲ ▲ ▲ ▲ ▲ ▲ ▲ ▲ ▲ ▲ ▲ ▲ ▲ ▲ ▲ ▲ ▲ ▲ ▲

1218. True or false? The Incredible Hulk was grey when he was first introduced.

1222. *The Adventures of Tintin* was created by artist Georges Remi. What was his pen name?

1225. The comic strip *Gasoline Alley* is famous for what innovation?
a. split panels
b. characters aging
c. no men were featured
d. speech bubbles

1223. What is the name of Tintin's dog?
a. Snowy
b. Sonny
c. Ziggy
d. Samson

1226. What is Garfield's favorite food?

1224. What is the name of the absent-minded professor in Tintin?
a. Professor Calculus
b. Professor Haddock
c. Professor Holmes
d. Professor Venkman

1227. What Middle Eastern city does Garfield continually attempt to send Nermal to?
a. Abu Dhabi
b. Baghdad
c. Dubai
d. Istanbul

Answers: 1215. c; 1216. Black Panther; 1217. d; 1218. true; 1219. false; 1220. d; 1221. Starfox; 1222. Hergé; 1223. a; 1224. a; 1225. b; 1226. lasagna; 1227. a

1228. In *Peanuts*, what is the relationship between Linus and Lucy?

1229. What is Snoopy's sleepy brother's name?

1230. What does Peppermint Patty call Charlie Brown?

1231. What position does Schroeder play on Charlie Brown's baseball team?

1232. Who is in love with Schroeder?

1233. True or false? In some foreign countries, *Peanuts* was renamed *Radishes*.

TOUGH TRIVIA CHALLENGE

1234. What is Charlie Brown's father's profession?
a. lawyer
b. barber
c. chef
d. butcher

1235. Where was Snoopy born?
a. Del Rey Puppy Farm
b. Dense Hills Puppy Farm
c. Daisy Hill Puppy Farm
d. Daisy Way Puppy Farm

1236. TRUE OR FALSE? LUCY ONCE PUT LINUS'S BLANKET THROUGH A PAPER SHREDDER AND SPREAD THE PIECES ACROSS THE ATLANTIC OCEAN.

Complete the Titles of These Peanuts TV Specials.

◆◆◆

1237. It's the Great _____, Charlie Brown

1238. You're in _____, Charlie Brown

1239. He's Your _____, Charlie Brown

1240. Play It _____, Charlie Brown

1241. You're Not _____, Charlie Brown

1242. There's No Time for _____, Charlie Brown

1243. It's the Easter _____, Charlie Brown

1244. Be My _____, Charlie Brown

1245. You're a Good _____, Charlie Brown

1246. It's Your First _____, Charlie Brown

1247. What a _____, Charlie Brown

1248. You're the _____, Charlie Brown

1249. She's a Good _____, Charlie Brown

1250. Life is a _____, Charlie Brown

1251. Someday You'll Find _____, Charlie Brown

1252. Is This _____, Charlie Brown

1253. Happy New _____, Charlie Brown

1254. It's the Girl in the Red _____, Charlie Brown

1255. Why, Charlie Brown, _____?

1256. It's Christmastime _____, Charlie Brown

1257. You're in the Super _____, Charlie Brown

1258. It Was the Best _____ Ever, Charlie Brown

1259. It's the Pied _____, Charlie Brown

1260. _____ Must be Traded, Charlie Brown

1261. I Want a _____ for Christmas, Charlie Brown

1262. Which has been running for longer, *General Hospital* or *The Simpsons*?

1263. True or false? **The Simpsons** was the first animated series made for prime-time network television.

1264. What major studio created Looney Tunes?
a. Columbia b. Paramount
c. Universal d. Warner Bros.

1265. True or false? Porky Pig was originally paired with a cat named Beans.

TOUGH TRIVIA CHALLENGE

1267. On *Scooby-Doo*, what is Shaggy's real name?
a. Bob Denver
b. Fred Jones
c. Lomez Newman
d. Norville Rogers

1266. In what decade was Bugs Bunny created?
a. 1930s
b. 1940s
c. 1950s
d. 1960s

1268. According to the theme song for SpongeBob SquarePants, "absorbent and yellow and _____ is he."

1273. Who was the first U.S. president to appear on television?

a. Franklin Roosevelt   **b. Harry Truman**

c. Dwight Eisenhower   **d. John F. Kennedy**

1274. Every episode of *Seinfeld* contains an image or reference to what superhero?

a. Batman   b. Iron Man

c. Spider-Man   d. Superman

Answers: 1262. *General Hospital*; 1263. false, *The Flintstones* was; 1264. d; 1265. true; 1266. a; 1267. d; 1268. porous; 1269. d; 1270. a; 1271. c; 1272. b; 1273. a; 1274. d

Cultural Cachet • **129**

1275. What was the maid's name on *The Brady Bunch*?
a. Alice   b. Carol
c. Cindy   d. Jan

1276. Academy Award-winning filmmaker Ron Howard starred as a child on which popular sitcom?
a. *The Andy Griffith Show*   b. *The Brady Bunch*
c. *The Cosby Show*   d. *The Honeymooners*

1277. Were there more episodes made of *Star Trek* or *Star Trek: The Next Generation*?

1278. What does ESPN stand for?

1279. WHAT DID AMC ORIGINALLY STAND FOR?

1280. What cable TV network made the claim, "It's not TV, it's _____."

MATCH THE BELOVED CHARACTER WITH THEIR SITCOM.

1281. Kramer	a. *Seinfeld*
1282. Steve Urkel	b. *Happy Days*
1283. Lowell Mather	c. *Family Matters*
1284. Minkus	d. *The Office*
1285. Dwight Schrute	e. *30 Rock*
1286. Mary Ann Summers	f. *Parks and Rec*
1287. Fez	g. *Friends*
1288. Fonzie	h. *That '70s Show*
1289. Phoebe Buffay	i. *Boy Meets World*
1290. Geoffrey	j. *Wings*
1291. Woody Boyd	k. *Three's Company*
1292. Radar O'Reilly	l. *Fresh Prince of Bel-Air*
1293. Ron Swanson	m. *Gilligan's Island*
1294. Mr. Roper	n. *Cheers*
1295. Liz Lemon	o. *M*A*S*H*

CHAPTER 4

Social Studies

ANCIENT HISTORY

1296. True or false? **The ancestors of humans mastered fire before the Sahara became a desert.**

1297. Which is greater, the height of the Great Pyramid or the length of one of its sides?

TOUGH TRIVIA CHALLENGE

1298. What was the estimated world population in 100,000 BCE?
a. 125,000
b. 1,250,000
c. 12,500,000
d. 125,000,000

1299. The _____ is the earliest known system of laws.
a. Code of Hammurabi
b. Dead Sea Scrolls
c. Rosetta Stone
d. Torah

1300. Nebuchadnezzar II built which of the seven wonders of the ancient world to please Queen Amytis?
a. The Colossus of Rhodes
b. The Lighthouse at Alexandria
c. The Hanging Gardens of Babylon
d. The Temple of Artemis at Ephesus

1301. WHERE DID ARABIC NUMERALS ORIGINATE?

1302. How many of the seven wonders of the ancient world still exist?

    a. 0

    b. 1

    c. 2

    d. 3

1303. True or false? The Ancient Egyptians used stones as pillows.

1304. True or false? Iron was once considered more valuable than gold.

1305. Who controlled most of the world in 500 BCE?

    a. Romans   b. Persians

    c. Aztecs   d. Greeks

1306. The Peloponnesian War was between which two Greek states?

1309. ON WHAT ISLAND DID ANCIENT GREEK CIVILIZATION ORIGINATE?
A. CRETE
B. DELOS
C. OLYMPIA
D. RHODES

1307. At what age did boys in ancient Sparta begin military school?
a. 4
b. 5
c. 6
d. 7

1310. Which Greek goddess was the Acropolis primarily dedicated to, Athena or Aphrodite?

1308. Galen was a famous Greek _____.
a. philosopher
b. playwright
c. politician
d. physician

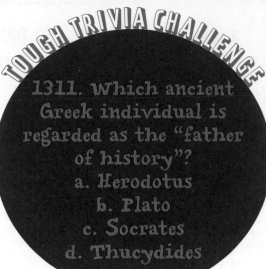

1311. Which ancient Greek individual is regarded as the "father of history"?
a. Herodotus
b. Plato
c. Socrates
d. Thucydides

1312. True or false? The great Carthaginian general Hannibal is the only individual to defeat the forces of Alexander the Great in battle.

▲▲▲▲▲▲▲▲▲▲▲▲▲▲▲

1313. True or false? After his death, Alexander the Great's body was preserved in honey for 3 years.

1314. WHO BURNED THE TEMPLE IN JERUSALEM IN THE YEAR 70 CE?
A. GREEKS
B. TURKS
C. ROMANS
D. EGYPTIANS

▲▲▲▲▲▲▲▲▲▲▲▲▲▲▲▲▲▲▲▲▲▲▲▲▲▲

1315. It has been said that Rome was founded by refugees from what war?
a. Macedonian
b. Peloponnesian
c. Punic
d. Trojan

1316. Which Roman emperor was once captured by pirates and held for ransom, Julius Caesar or Nero?

▲▲▲▲▲▲▲▲▲▲▲▲▲▲▲▲▲▲▲▲▲▲▲▲▲▲▲▲▲▲▲▲

1317. Was ancient Rome or Beijing the first city to reach a population of 1 million?

▲▲▲▲▲▲▲▲▲▲▲▲▲▲▲▲▲▲▲▲▲▲▲▲▲▲▲▲▲▲▲▲

1318. In imperial Rome, what was the highest social class?
a. Bourgeoisie
b. Patrician
c. Plebian
d. Proletarian

▲▲▲▲▲▲▲▲▲▲▲▲▲▲▲▲▲▲▲▲▲▲▲▲▲▲▲▲▲▲▲▲

1319. Which ancient empire had no written language?
a. Aztec   b. Incan
c. Persian   d. Roman

▲▲▲▲▲▲▲▲▲▲▲▲▲▲▲▲▲▲▲▲▲▲▲▲▲▲▲▲▲▲▲▲

Answers: 1311. a; 1312. false; Alexander's forces were never defeated; 1313. true; 1314. c; 1315. d; 1316. Julius Caesar; 1317. Rome; 1318. b; 1319. b

Social Studies • **137**

1320. What did the Aztecs use as money?

a. parrot feathers   b. stones

c. cocoa beans   d. sea shells

1321. How did Attila the Hun die on his wedding night?

a. nosebleed
b. poisoned
c. stabbed by his wife
d. trampled by zebras

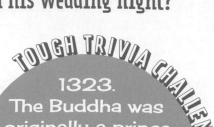

1323.
The Buddha was
originally a prince
named _____.
a. Siddhartha
b. Silmarion
c. Sidvicious
d. Siddeus

1322. Which was founded first, Buddhism or Christianity?

1324. In the search for a potion that would provide eternal life, what did Chinese alchemists stumble upon in the 9th century?

a. toothpaste   b. gunpowder

c. rubbing alcohol   d. stainless steel

1326. True or false? During the Middle Ages, religious leaders condemned forks because they believed food should only enter the body via hands.

TOUGH TRIVIA CHALLENGE

1325. True or false? To apologize to Pope Gregory for asking the Pope to step down, King Henry IV knelt down in the snow and kissed his toe.

1327. A plague known as the Black Death is estimated to have killed what percentage of Europe's population in the 14th century?

a. 25   b. 35   c. 45   d. 55

1328. TRUE OR FALSE? DEAD BODIES OF PLAGUE VICTIMS WERE HURLED AT ENEMIES VIA CATAPULT IN THE CRIMEA.

1329. How much did a suit of armor weigh in the early Middle Ages?

a. 10 to 40 pounds   b. 45 to 80 pounds
c. 90 to 110 pounds   d. 120 to 170 pounds

Answers: 1320. c; 1321. a; 1322. Buddhism; 1323. a; 1324. b; 1325. true; 1326. true; 1327. c; 1328. true; 1329. b.

Social Studies • 139

1330. Did the Hundred Years' War last for more or less than 100 years?

1331. Joan of Arc rallied the troops of which country in the Hundred Years' War, France or England?

TOUGH TRIVIA CHALLENGE

1332. In what century did French become the official language of France?
a. 13th   b. 14th
c. 15th   d. 16th

1333. Who was Leif Ericsson's father?
a. Eric the Blue
b. Eric the Green
c. Eric the Grey
d. Eric the Red

1334. Although Christopher Columbus was Italian, what country financed his expedition to the New World?

1335. True or false? On one trip to the New World, pirates sunk two of Christopher Columbus's ships in the Gulf of Mexico.

1336. When was Australia settled by Britain as a prison colony?
- a. 1452
- b. 1788
- c. 1822
- d. 1854

1338. Who was the first European explorer to see the Pacific Ocean?
- a. Vasco de Gama
- b. Christopher Columbus
- c. Vasco Nunez de Balboa
- d. Hernan Cortes

1339. WHO LANDED IN FLORIDA AND ESTABLISHED ST. AUGUSTINE WHILE SEARCHING FOR THE MYTHICAL FOUNTAIN OF YOUTH?
- A. HERNANDO DE SOTO
- B. JOHN CABOT
- C. SIR FRANCIS DRAKE
- D. JUAN PONCE DE LEON

1337. The continents North and South America are named for which famous Italian explorer?

Answers: 1330. more (116 years); 1331. France; 1332. d; 1333. d; 1334. Spain; 1335. false, Columbus never reached the Gulf of Mexico; 1336. b; 1337. Amerigo Vespucci; 1338. c; 1339. d

MATCH THE EUROPEAN EXPLORER TO THEIR DISCOVERY OR ACHIEVEMENT.

1340. ABEL TASMAN

1341. BARTOLOMEU DIAS

1342. VASCO DE GAMA

1343. FERDINAND MAGELLAN

1344. JACQUES CARTIER

1345. HERNANDO DE SOTO

A. FIRST TO SAIL AROUND THE CAPE OF GOOD HOPE

B. FIRST TO SAIL DIRECTLY FROM EUROPE TO INDIA

C. DISCOVERED NEW ZEALAND

D. DISCOVERED THE MISSISSIPPI RIVER

E. CIRCUMNAVIGATED THE GLOBE

F. CLAIMED CANADA FOR FRANCE

1346. How many passengers were aboard the Mayflower when it set sail in 1620?

a. 42   b. 72

c. 102   d. 132

1347. What tribe of Native Americans was the first to encounter the Pilgrims?

a. Cherokee   b. Mohican

c. Nauset   d. Pequot

1348. New York City began as a _____ colony.

a. Spanish   b. French

c. Dutch   d. English

1349. True or false? George Washington once served in the British militia.

TOUGH TRIVIA CHALLENGE

1350. What were the British coming to do when Paul Revere warned that they were on the way?

a. arrest Samuel Adams and John Hancock

b. burn Boston

c. confiscate colonists' horses

d. take over an armory

1351. Why was George Washington's original Inauguration Day postponed?

    a. bad weather   **b. illness**

    c. British attack   **d. travel**

1352. What fraction of a person did slaves originally count as in the U.S. Constitution?

    a. 1/8   b. 1/4

    c. 3/5   d. 3/4

1353. Which founding father is known for his large signature on the Declaration of Independence?

1355. Which president purchased the Louisiana Territory from France?

    a. John Adams

    b. Thomas Jefferson

    c. James Madison

    d. James Monroe

TOUGH TRIVIA CHALLENGE

1354. Who drafted the Bill of Rights before becoming president?

    a. George Washington

    b. Thomas Jefferson

    c. John Adams

    d. James Madison

1356. WHO KILLED ALEXANDER HAMILTON IN AN 1804 DUEL?

1357. WHO WAS THE PROSECUTOR IN THE TRIAL OF RICHARD LAWRENCE, THE FIRST MAN TO EVER TRY TO ASSASSINATE A U.S. PRESIDENT?
A. ALEXANDER HAMILTON
B. FRANCIS SCOTT KEY
C. JOHN JAY
D. FRANKLIN PIERCE

TOUGH TRIVIA CHALLENGE

1358. Which president implemented the Native American relocation policy that led to the Trail of Tears?
a. Thomas Jefferson
b. James Madison
c. Andrew Jackson
d. James Garfield

1359. True or false? Abraham Lincoln lost his run for the U.S. Senate in 1858, two years before he won the presidency.

1360. In 1905, U.S. President Theodore Roosevelt was awarded the Nobel Peace Prize after helping arrange a peace treaty between which two countries?
a. Japan and China
b. China and Russia
c. Russia and Japan
d. Peru and Argentina

Answers: 1351. a; 1352. c; 1353. c; 1354. d; 1355. b; 1356. Aaron Burr; 1357. b; 1358. c; 1359. true; 1360. c

1361. Which four presidents have their likenesses featured on Mount Rushmore?

1362. Which president is the only one to have served in two nonconsecutive terms?
a. George Washington
b. William McKinley
c. Andrew Jackson
d. Grover Cleveland

1363. Which president introduced Thanksgiving as a national holiday?
a. George Washington
b. John Adams
c. Abraham Lincoln
d. Theodore Roosevelt

1364. John F. Kennedy was assassinated in which Texas city?
A. Austin
B. Dallas
C. Houston
D. San Antonio

1365. Which president was elected to the office four times?

1366. Which president was in office for the shortest amount of time?

    a. Andrew Johnson   b. Chester A. Arthur

    c. William Henry Harrison   d. William McKinley

1367. What was Franklin Roosevelt's plan to lift the U.S. out of the Great Depression known as?

    a. Big Deal   b. Fair Deal
    c. New Deal   d. Nice Deal

1368. True or false? The S in Harry S. Truman stands for Simon.

1369. Which president signed the Civil Rights Act in 1964?

a. Dwight D. Eisenhower   b. John F. Kennedy
c. Lyndon B. Johnson   d. Richard Nixon

1370. Who is the only U.S. president that has resigned?

    a. Bill Clinton   **b. Richard Nixon**
    c. Rutherford B. Hayes   **d. Franklin Roosevelt**

1371. WHAT U.S. PRESIDENT ALSO SERVED AS THE CHIEF JUSTICE ON THE SUPREME COURT, JAMES MADISON, GROVER CLEVELAND, OR WILLIAM HOWARD TAFT?

1372. Which president was head of the U.S. Armed Forces in Europe during World War II?

1373. Which president had solar panels installed on the White House roof?
- a. Jimmy Carter
- b. Ronald Reagan
- c. Bill Clinton
- d. Donald Trump

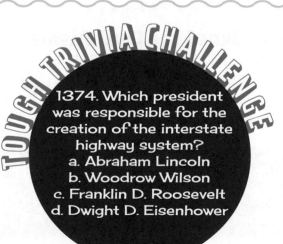

TOUGH TRIVIA CHALLENGE

1374. Which president was responsible for the creation of the interstate highway system?
- a. Abraham Lincoln
- b. Woodrow Wilson
- c. Franklin D. Roosevelt
- d. Dwight D. Eisenhower

1375. What president signed Martin Luther King Day into law?
- a. Richard Nixon
- b. Jimmy Carter
- c. Ronald Reagan
- d. Bill Clinton

MATCH THE PRESIDENT TO THEIR VICE PRESIDENT.

1376. Barack Obama	a. Andrew Johnson
1377. George W. Bush	b. Dick Cheney
1378. Ronald Reagan	c. Calvin Coolidge
1379. Jimmy Carter	d. Nelson Rockefeller
1380. Gerald Ford	e. John Adams
1381. Richard Nixon	f. Henry Wallace
1382. John F. Kennedy	g. Aaron Burr
1383. Dwight Eisenhower	h. George H.W. Bush
1384. Franklin D. Roosevelt	i. Lyndon B. Johnson
1385. Warren Harding	j. Thomas Jefferson
1386. William McKinley	k. Richard Nixon
1387. Abraham Lincoln	l. Walter Mondale
1388. Andrew Jackson	m. Spiro Agnew
1389. Thomas Jefferson	n. Joe Biden
1390. John Adams	o. Theodore Roosevelt
1391. George Washington	p. Martin Van Buren

Answers: 1371. William Howard Taft; 1372. Dwight D. Eisenhower; 1373. a; 1374. d; 1375. c; 1376. n; 1377. b; 1378. h; 1379. l; 1380. d; 1381. m; 1382. i; 1383. k; 1384. f; 1385. c; 1386. o; 1387. a; 1388. p; 1389. g; 1390. j; 1391. e.

Social Studies • 49

1392. The Statue of Liberty was a gift to the U.S. from what country?

- - - - - - -

1394. Which was the first state to secede from the Union preceding the Civil War?

    a. South Carolina
    b. Georgia
    c. Mississippi
    d. Alabama

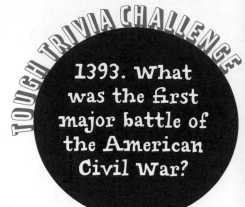

TOUGH TRIVIA CHALLENGE

1393. What was the first major battle of the American Civil War?

- - - - - - -

1395. Which of these Southern cities served as a capital of the Confederate States of America?

    a. Jackson, Mississippi
    b. New Orleans, Louisiana
    c. Charleston, South Carolina
    d. Richmond, Virginia

1396. TRUE OR FALSE? ROBERT E. LEE, THE TOP CONFEDERATE GENERAL, WAS ALSO OFFERED COMMAND OF THE UNION FORCES.

1397. WHAT WAS THE LEADING CAUSE OF DEATH AMONG SOLDIERS IN THE CIVIL WAR?

A. DISEASE   B. STARVATION
C. GUNSHOT WOUNDS   D. CANNON FIRE

1398. True or false? American Civil War general Ambrose Burnside started the fashion of wearing sideburns.

1399. True or false? Mississippi did not ratify the 13th Amendment, which abolished slavery, until 2013.

1400. Which state has the motto: "Live free or die."

a. Delaware   b. New Hampshire
c. Texas   d. Wisconsin

1401. What was the first state to approve the U.S. Constitution and enter the union?

a. Delaware
b. Massachusetts
c. New Hampshire
d. New York

Answers: 1392. France; 1393. The First Battle of Bull Run; 1394. a; 1395. d; 1396. true; 1397. a; 1398. true; 1399. true; 1400. b; 1401. a.

Social Studies • 151

1402. True or false? The U.S. has always imposed an income tax on its residents.

....

1403. Prohibition, which banned the sale and possession of alcohol, was enacted in _____.

a. 1910
b. 1915
c. 1920
d. 1925

....

1404. The 1920s are commonly known as "The _____ Twenties."

a. Booming
b. Boring
c. Dry
d. Roaring

....

1405. Bonnie and Clyde committed most of their crimes in the _____.

a. 1910s
b. 1920s
c. 1930s
d. 1940s

1406. Famous gangster Al Capone quit school after the _____.

a. 1st grade
b. 6th grade
c. 9th grade
d. 12th grade

....

1407. True or false? Al Capone once ran a soup kitchen for the poor of Chicago.

1408. THE GREAT CHICAGO FIRE AND WISCONSIN'S PESHTIGO FIRE BOTH OCCURRED ON THE SAME DAY IN 1871. WHICH NOTORIOUS FIRE RESULTED IN MORE DEATHS?

1409. Who was the first woman appointed to the Supreme Court?

    a. Ruth Bader Ginsburg
    b. Sandra Day O'Connor
    c. Elena Kagan
    d. Sonia Sotomayor

Were these Supreme Court justices ever Chief Justice (yes or no)?

1410. Harlan Stone

1411. Oliver Wendell Holmes

1412. Thurgood Marshall

1413. Earl Warren

1414. Warren Burger

1415. Byron White

1416. William Rehnquist

1417. Felix Frankfuter

1418. John Roberts

1419. Salmon Chase

1420. Antonin Scalia

1421. David Souter

1422. John Jay

1423. What year were Hawaii and Alaska granted statehood?

1424. What was the first U.S. state to make Labor Day a holiday?

Answers: 1402. false, the income tax did not become permanent until 1913; 1403; 1404. d; 1405. c; 1406. b; 1407. true; 1408. the Peshtigo Fire, which is the deadliest wildfire in American history; 1409. b; 1410. yes; 1411. no; 1412. no; 1413. yes; 1414. yes; 1415. no; 1416. yes; 1417. no; 1418. yes; 1419. yes; 1420. no; 1421. no; 1422. yes; 1423. 1959; 1424. Oregon

Social Studies • 153

1425. True or false? Napoleon was the leading figure behind the Reign of Terror during the French Revolution.

1426. Which country sent an enormous naval battalion known as the Armada to attack Britain in 1588?
a. France
b. Germany
c. Spain
d. Portugal

TOUGH TRIVIA CHALLENGE

1427. Who is Bolivia named after?

1428. The Treaty of Versailles followed which war?
a. Hundred Years' War
b. Crimean War
c. World War I
d. World War II

1429. Whose death in 1924 triggered a power struggle between Leon Trotsky and Joseph Stalin in the Soviet Union?
a. Leo Tolstoy
b. Nicholas II
c. Vladimir Lenin
d. Rasputin

1430. THE INDIAN METROPOLIS OF BOMBAY IS NOW KNOWN AS _____.

1431. When did India win its independence from England?

a. 1722　　b. 1810

c. 1887　　d. 1947

1432. Before becoming world famous as a political figure, Mohandas Gandhi was a _____.

a. doctor　　b. farmer

c. insurance agent　　d. lawyer

1433. Which famous military leader was once forced to retreat after being attacked by rabbits, Genghis Khan or Napoleon?

1434. In World War II, what was the name given to Germany's invasion strategy?

a. blitzkrieg　　b. kristallnacht

c. perestroika　　d. reich

Answers: 1425. false; 1426. c; 1427. Simon Bolivar, who liberated the country in 1824; 1428. c; 1429. c; 1430. Mumbai; 1431. d; 1432. d; 1433. Napoleon; 1434. a.

Social Studies • 155

1435. What German political leader was known as the "Iron Chancellor"?
a. Adolf Hitler
b. Kaiser Wilhelm
c. Otto von Bismarck
d. Willy Brandt

1436. Adolf Hitler was born in which country?
a. Austria
b. Germany
c. Hungary
d. Sweden

1437. The Battle of Midway was fought in which ocean?
a. Atlantic
b. Indian
c. Pacific
d. Southern

1438. What nations made up the Axis Powers in World War II?
a. Spain, Italy, and Germany
b. Germany, Italy, and Japan
c. Germany, Russia, and Spain
d. Germany, Japan, and Russia

1439. What World War II general was known as the "Desert Fox"?
a. Hideki Tojo
b. Erich von Manstein
c. George Patton
d. Erwin Rommel

1440. THE D-DAY INVASION TOOK PLACE IN WHAT FRENCH REGION?
A. NORMANDY
B. COGNAC
C. BRITTANY
D. PROVENCE

1441. What is the name of the British national anthem?

1442. What British prime minister was also known as "The Iron Lady"?

1443. Which Academy Award-winning actress portrayed "The Iron Lady" in a film by that name, Helen Mirren or Meryl Streep?

1444. True or false? Albert Einstein was offered the role of Israel's second president in 1952?

1446. What disastrous economic program did Chinese leader Mao Zedong announce in 1958?

a. The Enlightened Transformation

b. The Great Leap Forward

c. The Workers' Awakening

d. Voodoo Economics

TOUGH TRIVIA CHALLENGE

1445. What tangled international affair involved forces from China, Japan, Russia, Britain, France, the United States, Germany, Italy, and Austria-Hungary?
a. Boxer Rebellion
b. Dreyfus Affair
c. Taiping Rebellion
d. none of the above

Answers: 1435. c; 1436. a; 1437. c; 1438. b; 1439. d; 1440. a; 1441. God Save the Queen; 1442. Margaret Thatcher; 1443. Meryl Streep; 1444. true; 1445. a; 1446. b

Social Studies • 157

1447. How many years did Nelson Mandela spend in prison before becoming president of South Africa?

a. 3
b. 9
c. 18
d. 27

1448. FIDEL CASTRO AND WHICH FAMOUS REVOLUTIONARY WERE KEY FIGURES IN THE CUBAN REVOLUTION?

A. ANDRES BONIFACIO
B. CHE GUEVARA
C. JOHN REED
D. SURYA SEN

1449. The Khmer Rouge ruled in which Asian nation during the 20th century?

a. Cambodia
b. Laos
c. Thailand
d. Vietnam

1450. True or false? **The Dead Sea is below sea level.**

1451. Is the Bay of Fundy on the Atlantic or Pacific coast of North America?

Match the national park to the state it is in.

1452. Glacier Bay   a. New Mexico

1453. Crater Lake   b. Oregon

1454. Carlsbad Caverns   c. Washington

1455. Mount Rainier   d. Alaska

1456. TRUE OR FALSE? AUSTRALIA WAS ONCE CONNECTED TO ANTARCTICA, INDIA, AND AFRICA AS PART OF A SUPER CONTINENT NOW KNOWN AS GONDWANALAND.

Answers: 1447. d; 1448. b; 1449. d; 1450. true; 1451. Atlantic; 1452. d; 1453. b; 1454. a; 1455. c; 1456. true.

Social Studies • 159

MATCH THE COUNTRY TO ITS FORMER NAME.

▲▲▲▲▲▲▲▲▲▲▲▲▲▲▲▲▲▲▲▲▲▲▲▲▲▲▲▲▲▲▲▲

1457. ZIMBABWE

1458. VIETNAM

1459. THAILAND

1460. CAMBODIA

1461. MYANMAR

1462. IRAN

1463. ETHIOPIA

1464. SRI LANKA

A. KAMPUCHEA

B. SIAM

C. CEYLON

D. ABYSSINIA

E. RHODESIA

F. PERSIA

G. FRENCH INDOCHINA

H. BURMA

1465. What is the largest continent?

1466. What is the largest country (by square miles) in Africa?
   a. Algeria
   b. Egypt
   c. Kenya
   d. South Africa

1467. Is it the Euphrates River or the Tigris River that runs through Baghdad, Iraq?

TOUGH TRIVIA CHALLENGE

1469. What African country served as the setting for Tatooine in Star Wars?
   a. Ethiopia
   b. Ghana
   c. Kenya
   d. Tunisia

1468. Machu Picchu can be found in what South American country?
   a. Colombia
   b. Chile
   c. Peru
   d. Uruguay

Answers: 1457. e; 1458. g; 1459. b; 1460. a; 1461. h; 1462. f; 1463. d; 1464. c; 1465. Asia; 1466. a; 1467. Tigris River; 1468. c; 1469. d

Social Studies • **161**

1470. What country is Mount Everest in?

1471. What American mountain is actually taller than Mount Everest if you measure it from its base?

1472. Two days before Edmund Hillary and Tenzing Norgay made it to the top of Everest in 1953, Tom Bourdillon and Charles Evans were close to the top, but they ran out of oxygen and turned back around. How close were they to the top?

    a. 100 feet
    b. 300 feet
    c. 700 feet
    d. 1200 feet

1473. True or false? Both Annapurna and K2 are considered more dangerous mountains to climb than Mount Everest.

1474. WHICH IS HIGHER: KILIMANJARO IN TANZANIA OR DENALI IN THE U.S.?

1475. On what continent are the Andes?

1476. On what continent are the San Bernardino Mountains?

1477. California's Mt. Shasta is a potentially active _____.

1478. The Appalachian Mountains stretch from Alabama to which Canadian province?

1479. True or false? Approximately half of the world's population lives within 60 miles of an ocean.

TOUGH TRIVIA CHALLENGE

1480. What is the largest island on Earth, Greenland or Madagascar?

1481. In what U.S. state does the Mississippi River begin?
a. Minnesota
b. Michigan
c. Wisconsin
d. Ohio

1482. TRUE OR FALSE? NO ONE HAS EVER SWUM THE ENTIRE LENGTH OF THE MISSISSIPPI RIVER.

1483. True or false? The Mississippi River once served as the border between the Spanish Empire and the British Empire.

1484. What is the longest river in Asia?

1485. True or false? There are porpoises in the Yangtze River.

1486. What is the longest river in Europe, the Danube or the Volga?

1487. What is larger, a creek or a stream?

1488. What is larger, a channel or a sound?

1489. What is the name of the spot where a fresh waterway empties into a body of salt water?

a. bay

b. estuary

c. isthmus

d. sound

1490. What Ohio waterway once caught on fire due to pollution?
a. Cuyahoga River
b. Mad River
b. Ohio River
d. Scioto River

1491. In what U.S. state is Catalina Island?

1492. TRUE OR FALSE? THERE ARE MORE THAN 30.000 ISLANDS IN THE GREAT LAKES.

1493. Which Great Lake is the source of the St. Lawrence River?
a. Lake Huron
b. Lake Ontario
c. Lake Michigan
d. Lake Superior

1494. Which is larger, Africa's Lake Victoria or North America's Lake Superior?

1495. Is Egypt at the source or the mouth of the Nile River?

TOUGH TRIVIA CHALLENGE

1497. What is the longest bridge over water in the United States?
a. Tappan Zee Bridge
b. Lake Pontchartrain Causeway
c. Chesapeake Bay Bridge
d. Golden Gate Bridge

1496. True or false? There are no bridges that cross the Amazon River.

MATCH THE CITY TO THE RIVER IT IS ON THE BANKS OF.

1498. Cincinnati   **a. Danube**

1499. Dusseldorf   **b. Rhine**

1500. Yonkers   **c. Ohio**

1501. Vienna   **d. Hudson**

1502. What Western U.S. city was awarded the 1976 Winter Olympics but refused?
  - a. Denver
  - b. Missoula
  - c. Reno
  - d. Salt Lake City

1503. What U.S. state is known as the Volunteer State?
  - a. Kentucky
  - b. Tennessee
  - c. Texas
  - d. Virginia

1504. What U.S. state is known as the Magnolia State?
  - a. Alabama
  - b. Georgia
  - c. Mississippi
  - d. South Carolina

1505. In addition to being a tourist attraction, the Taj Mahal is also a _____.
  - a. hotel
  - b. mausoleum
  - c. school
  - d. office building

1506. Buenos Aires is the capital of what South American country?

1507. Which of the following is not one of the official languages of Belgium?
  - a. Belgian
  - b. French
  - c. German
  - d. Dutch

Answers: 1494, Lake Superior; 1495, mouth; 1496, true; 1497, b; 1498, c; 1499, b; 1500, d; 1501, a; 1502, a; 1503, a; 1504, c; 1505, b; 1506, Argentina; 1507, a

Social Studies • 167

1508. In what country would you find the cities Glasgow and Edinburgh?

1510. Istanbul in Turkey was known as _____ until 1924.

1509. What is the largest country, by size and population, in South America?

1511. Port-au-Prince is the capital of what Caribbean nation?

1512. TRUE OR FALSE? ANNAPOLIS, MARYLAND ONCE SERVED AS THE CAPITAL OF THE UNITED STATES.

1513. True or false? Boston, Massachusetts once served as the capital of the United States.

1514. WHAT IS THE CAPITAL OF AUSTRALIA?
A. CANBERRA   B. MELBOURNE
C. SYDNEY   D. PERTH

1515. What is the only continent with land in all four hemispheres?
a. Africa
b. Antarctica
c. Asia
d. Australia

TOUGH TRIVIA CHALLENGE

1516. Spain, France, and which African nation are the only three countries to have both Atlantic and Mediterranean coastlines?
a. Egypt
b. Libya
c. Morocco
d. South Africa

1517. Which major city is located on two continents, Istanbul or Moscow?

1518. What is the world's deepest lake, Lake Baikal or Lake Superior?

Answers: 1508. Scotland; 1509. Brazil; 1510. Haiti; 1511. Constantinople; 1512. true; 1513. false; 1514. a; 1515. a; 1516. c; 1517. Istanbul; 1518 Lake Baikal, which has a maximum depth of 5,387 feet and contains more water than all of the Great Lakes combined.

Social Studies • **169**

CHAPTER 5

Trivia Salad

1519. True or false? **A food must contain no sugar in order to be called "sugar free."**

1520. Soft-serve ice cream involves increasing the amount of _____?

a. air   b. egg

c. milk   d. sugar

Match the Latin name to the fruit.

1521. citrullius lanatus
1522. rubes idaeus
1523. cocus nucifera
1524. malus sylvestris
1525. prunus persica
1526. phoenix dactylifera
1527. ananas comosus
1528. prunus armeniaca
1529. citrus sinensis
1530. rheum rharbararum

a. raspberry
b. orange
c. watermelon
d. pineapple
e. rhubarb
f. apricot
g. peach
h. apple
i. coconut
j. fig

WEIGHT LOSS PROGRAM

1531. True or false? Goat's milk is OK to consume on a vegan diet.

- - - - - - - - -

1532. What provides the crunch in a Nestle Crunch bar?
    a. almonds b. puffed wheat
    c. rice   d. corn

- - - - - - -

1533. True or false? Per person, Germans consume twice as much candy a year as Americans.

- - - - - - - - -

1534. True or false? Candy corn is the top-selling candy in the U.S.

- - - - - - - - -

1535. True or false? Gum is not digestible by the human body.

- - - - - - - -

1536. True or false? U.S. president Richard Nixon regularly ate a Milky Way bar for breakfast.

- - - - - - - - -

1537. Which candy bar is named after the inventor's horse, Snickers or Butterfinger?

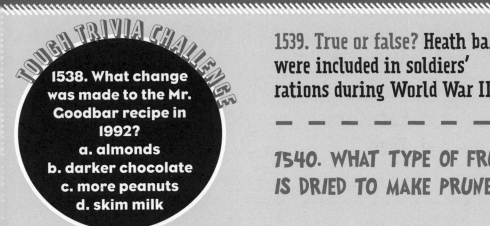

1538. What change was made to the Mr. Goodbar recipe in 1992?
a. almonds
b. darker chocolate
c. more peanuts
d. skim milk

1539. True or false? Heath bars were included in soldiers' rations during World War II.

1540. WHAT TYPE OF FRUIT IS DRIED TO MAKE PRUNES?

1541. Pizza as we know it is believed to have been conceived in which city?
a. Naples, Italy
b. New Haven, Connecticut
c. Rome, Italy
d. New York, New York

1542. What condiment can be used to shine copper?

1543. Before it was the perfect partner for hot dogs, mustard was a _____.
a. medicine
b. motor oil
c. paint
d. none of the above

1544. Which of the following is not a kind of apple?
a. McIntosh   b. Cortland   c. Green Delicious   d. Winesap

Answers: 1531. false; 1532. c; 1533. true; 1534. true; 1535. false; 1536. true; 1537. Snickers; 1538. c; 1539. true; 1540. plums; 1541. a; 1542. ketchup; 1543. a; 1544. c.

Trivia Salad • 173

1545. Which of the following is not a kind of orange?
- a. Valencia
- b. Blood
- c. Cara Cara
- d. Peru

1546. Hot peppers are rated according to _____ heat units.
- a. Bell
- b. Kelvin
- c. Martinez
- d. Scoville

1547. True or false? The human body can digest fiber.

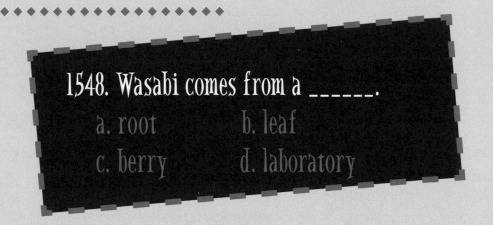

1548. Wasabi comes from a _____.
- a. root
- b. leaf
- c. berry
- d. laboratory

1549. TRUE OR FALSE? MOST WASABI IN THE UNITED STATES IS ACTUALLY HORSERADISH, MUSTARD, AND FOOD COLORING.

1550. Which of the following is an ingredient in a California sushi roll?

> a. avocado
> b. mango
> c. peach
> d. pineapple

◆◆◆◆◆◆◆◆◆◆◆◆◆◆◆◆◆

1552. Wheaties is "The Breakfast of _____."

1551. A fried burrito is known as a _____.
> a. chilaquile
> b. chimichanga
> c. quesadilla
> d. tostada

◆◆◆◆◆◆◆◆◆◆◆◆◆◆◆◆◆◆◆◆◆◆◆◆◆

1553. Who was the first athlete to be featured on a box of Wheaties?

> a. Jesse Owens
> b. Lou Gehrig
> c. Doug Flutie
> d. Michael Jordan

1554. When did the first McDonald's restaurant open?

  a. 1933   b. 1940

  c. 1949   d. 1954

1555. What was Col. Sanders first name?

  a. Alphonse   b. Jamison

  c. Quentin   d. Harland

1556. HOW MANY HERBS AND SPICES ARE IN THE SECRET BLEND THAT IS USED IN KFC'S ORIGINAL KFC BLEND?

  A. 5   B. 7   C. 9   D. 11

1557. True or false? Papa John's Pizza was founded in a broom closet.

1558. True or false? Fast food was initially called the "Speedee Service System."

1559. The forerunner of Taco Bell, Bell's Drive-In, specialized in what?

    a. fried chicken
    b. hamburgers
    c. hot dogs
    d. milkshakes

1560. Which has more locations as of 2018, McDonald's or Subway?

1561. Which great American novel is the inspiration of the name "Starbucks"?

    a. *Infinite Jest*
    b. *On the Road*
    c. *The Sun Also Rises*
    d. *Moby-Dick*

1562. In the John Mellencamp song "Jack and Diane," the title characters are enjoying a chili dog outside of which fast food restaurant?

    a. Hardee's
    b. Dairy Queen
    c. Tastee Freeze
    d. KFC

1563. What fast food chain is credited with introducing the drive-through window?

    a. Burger King
    b. Hardee's
    c. McDonald's
    d. Wendy's

MATCH THE FAMOUS MENU ITEM TO THE FAST FOOD RESTAURANT.

1564. JAMOCHA SHAKES

1565. FROSTY

1566. BLIZZARD

1567. DOUBLE-DOUBLE

1568. WHOPPER

1569. MUNCHKINS

1570. THE FAMOUS STAR

1571. THE CRAVE CASE

1572. THE BOOTLEGGER CLUB

1573. FILET-O-FISH

1574. BUTTERBURGER

1575. FRISCO MELT

1576. HONEY BUTTER CHICKEN BISCUIT

A. WHITE CASTLE

B. IN-N-OUT

C. DAIRY QUEEN

D. WHATABURGER

E. CARL'S JR.

F. DUNKIN' DONUTS

G. STEAK 'N SHAKE

H. MCDONALD'S

I. JIMMY JOHN'S

J. WENDY'S

K. BURGER KING

L. CULVER'S

M. ARBY'S

1577. What was the first fast food restaurant in China, Kentucky Fried Chicken, McDonald's, or Subway?

▲▲▲▲▲▲▲▲▲▲▲▲▲▲▲▲▲

1579. Which soft drink was produced first in the U.S?

    a. Coca-Cola   b. Dr. Pepper
    c. Pepsi   d. Sprite

TOUGH TRIVIA CHALLENGE

1578. What does the TGI in TGI Friday's stand for?

▲▲▲▲▲▲▲▲▲▲▲▲▲▲▲▲▲▲▲▲▲▲▲

1580. True or false? **Mountain Dew was initially invented to use as a mixer for whiskey.**

▲▲▲▲▲▲▲▲▲▲▲▲▲▲▲▲▲▲▲▲▲

1581. Kosher for Passover Coca-Cola contains _____ instead of high-fructose corn syrup.

a. fructose   **b. maple syrup**
c. sucrose   **d. honey**

▲▲▲▲▲▲▲▲▲▲▲▲▲▲▲▲▲▲▲▲

1582. What part of China does Cantonese cuisine come from?
    a. North **b. East**   **c. South** **d. West**

Match the cuisine to the signature dish.

1583. Canadian	a. haggis
1584. French	b. samosa
1585. German	c. paella
1586. Greek	d. baklava
1587. Hungarian	e. kimchi
1588. Indian	f. jerk chicken
1589. Irish	g. champ
1590. Italian	h. borscht
1591. Jamaican	i. goulash
1592. Japanese	j. crème brulee
1593. Korean	k. miso soup
1594. Mexican	l. hummus
1595. Middle Eastern	m. banh mi
1596. Moroccan	n. sauerbraten
1597. Polish	o. pierogi
1598. Russian	p. taco
1599. Scottish	q. poutine
1600. Southern	r. chicken tagine
1601. Spanish	s. hoppin' john
1602. Vietnamese	t. lasagna

1603. What is deer meat known as?

1604. True or false? Beefsteak is a variety of tomato.

1605. Is a pineapple considered a berry, a stone fruit, or a nut?

1606. Is a kumquat a stone fruit or a citrus fruit?

1607. Bread that is unleavened has no _____.

    a. salt

    b. water

    c. yeast

    d. none of the above

TOUGH TRIVIA CHALLENGE

1608. During the 1930s, a law in Wisconsin required restaurants to serve _____ with every meal.
a. bread and water
b. cheese and butter
c. milk and honey
d. salt and pepper

1609. WHAT SHAPE IS PENNE PASTA?

1610. If a dish is served "Florentine," it will be served with what?

    a. broccoli

    b. parsley

    c. spinach

    d. zucchini

Answers: 1583. q; 1584. j; 1585. n; 1586. d; 1587. i; 1588. b; 1589. g; 1590. c; 1591. f; 1592. k; 1593. e; 1594. p; 1595. l; 1596. r; 1597. o; 1598. h; 1599. a; 1600. s; 1601. l; 1602. m; 1603. venison; 1604. true; 1605. a berry; 1606. citrus fruit; 1607. c; 1608. b; 1609. tube-shaped; 1610. c.

Trivia Salad • **181**

2014

1611. What deadly disease became a global health crisis?
- a. avian flu
- b. Ebola
- c. mumps
- d. typhoid

1612. Sony Pictures had its computers hacked by which country?
- a. China
- b. North Korea
- c. Russia
- d. United States

1613. What artist's album *1989* sold more than a million copies in its first week?
- a. Beyonce
- b. Miley Cyrus
- c. Taylor Swift
- d. Kanye West

1614. Apple purchased Beats from which hip-hop legend?
- a. Dr. Dre
- b. Jay-Z
- c. Puff Daddy
- d. Snoop Dogg

1615. A hologram featuring which music great performed at the Billboard Music Awards?
- a. Marvin Gaye
- b. Michael Jackson
- c. Elvis Presley
- d. Otis Redding

1616. The Winter Olympics were held in Sochi, a city in which country?
- a. Finland
- b. Korea
- c. Japan
- d. Russia

1617. Led by Shabazz Napier, which college defeated Kentucky to win the NCAA men's basketball title, Texas or UConn?

1618. Which Yankees star played his final game in pinstripes, Derek Jeter or Mariano Rivera?

1619. Who won the NBA MVP?
- a. Kevin Durant
- b. James Harden
- c. LeBron James
- d. Russell Westbrook

1620. Who went wire-to-wire to win the British Open, Rory McIlroy or Phil Mickelson?

1621. Lionel Messi and Argentina were defeated by _____ in the World Cup final.
- a. Brazil
- b. France
- c. Germany
- d. Spain

2015

1622. Justin Trudeau was elected the prime minister of Canada in October. What job did Trudeau previously hold?

a. banker   b. doctor   c. lawyer   d. school teacher

1623. A massive, 7.8-magnitude earthquake struck near Kathmandu, _____.

a. India   b. Nepal   c. Thailand   d. Vietnam

Answers: 1611. b; 1612. b; 1613. c; 1614. a; 1615. b; 1616. d; 1617. UConn; 1618. Derek Jeter; 1619. a; 1620. Rory McIlroy; 1621. c; 1622. d; 1623. b.

Trivia Salad • 183

1624. NASA discovered Kepler 452b, a planet which is very similar to _ _ _ _ _ _.
a. Earth   b. Jupiter
c. Saturn   d. the Moon

1625. What was found on Mars, flowing water or fossilized plants?

1626. Which late-night host retired after more than three decades on television, Jay Leno or David Letterman?

1627. Which *Star Trek* star passed away, Leonard Nimoy or William Shatner?

1628. Thanks to the single _ _ _ _ _ _ _, Adele's 25 was the top-selling album.

1629. Bruno Mars and what super producer had a No. 1 hit with "Uptown Funk"?
a. Jeff Bhasker   b. Phil Ek
c. Max Martin   d. Mark Ronson

1630. Tom Brady was involved in what scandal following the AFC Championship?

1631. Which quarterback threw an interception on the 1 in the final moments of Super XLIX?
a. Tom Brady   b. Peyton Manning
c. Philip Rivers   d. Russell Wilson

1632. This Western Conference guard won the first of two straight NBA MVPs.

1633. Duke beat which college to win the men's NCAA championship, Kentucky or Wisconsin?

1634. Who defeated Japan to win the Women's World Cup in soccer?
a. Brazil   b. Canada
c. Germany   d. United States

1635. Which longtime leader of Cuba passed away?

◆ ◆ ◆ ◆ ◆ ◆ ◆ ◆ ◆ ◆ ◆ ◆ ◆ ◆ ◆

1636. Britain voted to leave the European Union in June, a move that was nicknamed _____.

a. Brexit   b. Brit Split
c. Eur-out   d. Isle-See-You

◆ ◆ ◆ ◆ ◆ ◆ ◆ ◆ ◆ ◆ ◆ ◆ ◆ ◆ ◆

1637. Donald Trump defeated _____ to win the U.S. presidency.

1638. His performance in *The Revenant* earned which actor his first Academy Award?

    a. Matt Damon
    b. Leonardo DiCaprio
    c. Tom Hardy
    d. Brad Pitt

1639. What actress paired with Ryan Gosling in *La La Land*?

a. Jennifer Lawrence   b. Blake Lively
c. Emma Stone   d. Michelle Williams

TOUGH TRIVIA CHALLENGE

1640. Beyonce's sister _____ had a hit album with *A Seat at the Table.*

1641. Which artist, also known as "Ziggy Stardust," passed away in January?

◆ ◆ ◆ ◆ ◆ ◆ ◆ ◆ ◆ ◆ ◆ ◆ ◆ ◆ ◆

1642. What legendary American songwriter won the Nobel Prize for Literature?

a. Fiona Apple
b. Bob Dylan
c. Eddie Vedder
d. Stevie Wonder

1643. Which record-breaking app was released in July, A Good Snowman is Hard to Build or Pokémon Go?

1644. Which MLB team won the World Series to end the longest championship drought in sports?

1645. Which gymnast won three individual gold medals at the Summer Olympics, Simone Biles or Gabby Douglas?

1646. Who hit the game-winning shot in Game 7 of the NBA Finals?
a. Steph Curry
b. Kyrie Irving
c. LeBron James
d. Klay Thompson

1647. Which 49ers quarterback garnered attention for kneeling during the national anthem?

2017

1648. The "Great American Eclipse" occurred within which month?
a. May   b. June   c. July   d. August

1649. What was the highest-grossing film worldwide, Star Wars: The Last Jedi or The Fate of the Furious?

1650. Prince Harry and American actress _____ announced that they were engaged in November.

1651. Actress Gal Gadot and director Patty Jenkins powered which movie to more than $800 million in earnings worldwide?

1652. After winning the Australian Open, Serena Williams missed the next three majors due to _____.
a. a knee injury   b. pregnancy
c. suspension   d. vacation

1653. Which college basketball powerhouse made its first Final Four?
a. Gonzaga
b. Syracuse
c. Wake Forest
d. Xavier

1654. Who won the NCAA women's basketball title, Notre Dame, South Carolina, or UConn?

1655. _ _ _ _ _ _ _ won his record 10th French Open title.
a. Novak Djokovic
b. Roger Federer
c. Rafael Nadal
d. Andy Murray

1656. WHICH UFC STAR BATTLED FLOYD MAYWEATHER JR. IN "THE MONEY FIGHT"?

1657. The IOC banned which country from the 2018 Winter Olympics?
a. China
b. North Korea
c. Russia
d. United States

1658. The 50th anniversary is the

_ _ _ _ _ _.

    a. diamond anniversary
    b. golden anniversary
    c. paper anniversary
    d. sugar anniversary

1659. Is Canadian Thanksgiving in October or December?

1660. How many hours are there in a week?

1661. The first reported incident of costumed kids in the U.S. asking for candy on Halloween was in what year?
    a. 1843
    b. 1911
    c. 1941
    d. 1973

Match the holiday to the month it is celebrated in.

1662. All Saints' Day	**a.** January
1663. Bastille Day	**b.** February
1664. Boxing Day	**c.** March
1665. St. Patrick's Day	**d.** April
1666. Epiphany	**e.** May
1667. Presidents' Day	**f.** June
1668. Mother's Day	**g.** July
1669. Earth Day	**h.** November
1670. Flag Day	**i.** December

1671. How many months end in the letter h?

1672. What is the name of the famous groundhog in Pennsylvania who sees or doesn't see his shadow?

1673. What city is Harvard in?

1674. What city is Yale in?

1675. What city is Dartmouth in?

1676. What city is Johns Hopkins in?

1677. Which English university was founded first, Oxford or Cambridge?

1678. WHAT DOES ESP STAND FOR?

1679. What does ICU stand for?

1680. What does POW stand for?

MATCH THE JOB TO THE WORK PERFORMED.

▲▲▲▲▲▲▲▲▲▲▲▲▲▲▲▲▲▲▲▲▲▲▲▲▲▲▲▲▲▲

1681. GROOM

A. MAKES STRINGED INSTRUMENTS

1682. MILLINER

B. MAKES SHOES

1683. COLLIER

C. MAKES ARROWS

1684. WAINWRIGHT

D. MAKES CANDLES

1685. COOPER

E. MAKES AND SELLS CHARCOAL

1686. CHANDLER

F. MAKES OR SELLS WOMEN'S HATS

1687. FLETCHER

G. WORKS WITH STONE

1688. MASON

H. MAKES BARRELS

1689. COBBLER

I. PUTS ON HORSESHOES

1690. FARRIER

J. CARES FOR HORSES

1691. LUTHIER

K. MAKES WAGONS

1692. Does the phrase tabula rasa mean blank slate or dinner table?

1693. What is the top color in the rainbow?
a. blue   b. green
c. orange   d. red

▲▲▲▲▲▲▲▲▲▲▲▲▲▲

1694. Which color is vermilion a shade of?
a. blue   b. green
c. red   d. yellow

▲▲▲▲▲▲▲▲▲▲▲▲▲▲

1695. Jonquil is a shade of what color?
a. blue   b. green
c. red   d. yellow

1696. TRUE OR FALSE? THE BARBIE DOLL WAS NAMED AFTER THE INVENTOR'S DAUGHTER.

▲▲▲▲▲▲▲▲▲▲▲▲▲▲

1697. Which rock band takes their name from UFOs that World War II pilots reported?
a. Foo Fighters b. Led Zeppelin
c. U2   d. The Who

▲▲▲▲▲▲▲▲▲▲▲▲▲▲

1698. What monster did a British representative claim to see while living in Nepal in 1832?

▲▲▲▲▲▲▲▲▲▲▲▲▲▲

1699. What famous monster has an NHL team named after it?

▲▲▲▲▲▲▲▲▲▲▲▲▲▲

1700. How many millimeters are there in 1 centimeter, 10 or 100?

Answers: 1681. j; 1682. f; 1683. e; 1684. k; 1685. h; 1686. d; 1687. c; 1688. g; 1689. b; 1690. i; 1691. a; 1692. blank slate; 1693. d; 1694. c; 1695. d; 1696. true; 1697. a; 1698. Abominable Snowman; 1699. Jersey Devil; 1700. 10